The Heart & the Rose

The Battle of Linlithgow Bridge 1526

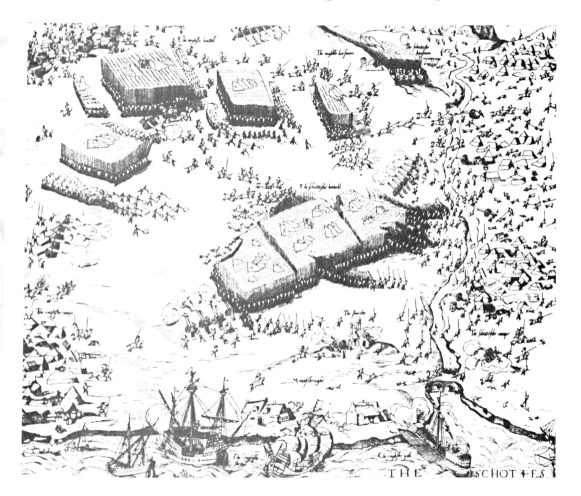

by
Jonathan Cooper

With illustrations by Alan Gault

PARTIZAN PRESS

Published by Partizan Press 2004
816 - 818 London Road, Leigh-on-sea,
Essex, SS9 3NH
Ph/Fx: +44 (0) 1702 473986
Email: ask@caliverbooks.com
www.caliverbooks.com

First published in Great Britain 2005 by
Partizan Press

Design & Production by Jay Forster

ISBN: 1-85818-523-8

Printed in Malta by Progress Press Ltd

Front Page:
'A Douglas' - Battle of Linlithgow Bridge' by Alan Gault
© Alan Gault 2005

Previous Page:
The Battle of Pinkie
© Edinburgh Central Public Library

Back Page:
Cleanse the Causey
© Alan Gault 2005

OTHER PARTIZAN HISTORICAL TITLES:

1 The Origins and Development of Military Tartans
James D Scarlett

2 The Last Scots Army 1661-1714
Stuart Reid

3 The Armies and Uniforms of Marlborough's Wars Pt1
CS Grant

4 The Armies and Uniforms of Marlborough's Wars Pt2
CS Grant

5 Cossack Hurrah! - Russian Irregular Cavalry Organisation
and Uniforms During the Napoleonic Wars
Dr S Summerfield

6 The King's Ships - Henry VIII's Royal Navy
Jonathan Davies

Partizan Special Edition series:
1 Sieges and Fortifications of the Civil Wars in Britain
Mike Osborne

Partizan Army Guides series:
1 The Organization of the Texan Army
Stuart Reid

COMING SOON

Russian Opolchenie of the Napoleonic Wars
Dr S Summerfield

British Cavalry in the Mid-18th Century
David Blackmore

Partizan Press Guide to Solo Wargaming
Stuart Asquith

Partizan Battledress series:
Alexander's Persian Battles
William Guthrie

Piedmontese Light Infantry and Bersaglieri
Luigi Casali

CONTENTS

Acknowledgements

I started researching this book in Jan 2003 when the members of the Gaddgedlar Re-enactment Society were looking for a local and unique presentation for the big Historic Scotland event at the Palace. I'm sure if I worked full time on the project in isolation. I would have cracked this book in 6 months. However life isn't like that and to get this project this far whilst holding down a day job, trying to be a husband to my long suffering wife Alison and father to my children has meant many people have been asked to tolerate my hobby.

In no particular order therefore I would like to mention a number of those stalwarts

Alan Gault, the illustrator of the book, has brought to life the characters and soldiery of the book. Alan was the main reason I started the project in the first place as he booked the Linlithgow Palace slot for Gadd and asked me to pull something together. He and the Gadd guys have provided the moving mannequins for the re-enactment shots. The accuracy of their recreation is second to none. I hope the unique experience they gave me in wearing this kit, and what more fighting in it, has come through in the account.

Nick Finnigan and Historic Scotland continue to support my efforts to bring this battle to the public. Not only are they custodians of many of the sites mentioned in the book but they have provided venues for the presentations, a mine of information about the properties and possible home for future finds and displays.

Tony Pollard and the GUARD team at Glasgow University have added that touch of professionalism and kudos to the project. They have continued to support all my efforts to research the site and put up with my insane ramblings and an amateurish concern with every chunk of metal I have pulled out of the ground to date. We are looking forward to a proper survey of the site in the near future, funding permitting

Cris Clelland who revealed the most exciting of finds from her bathroom and to all the other Black Bitches who have offered advice, guidance and oral history.

And to David Brodie and the Erskine's of Woodcockdale who let me poke around their land with metal detectors. A special thanks goes to RMC who have also provided permission to go onto the quarry site. These folk are the current guardians of the site and I hope this book will strengthen their resolve to ensure the battlefield is properly protected in the future.

Thanks to Jay and Dave at Partizan for bringing the book into being. For believing someone might be interested in reading it

Jamie Cameron and Caroline Bingham whose accounts of the life and reign of James were inspirational and to Douglas Paterson whose history of the period is second to none

Finally my family; Alison, Emily and the new mini Cooper, Adam who put in an appearance as this book went to press. Their patience, tolerance and support in what at times must have seemed like an obsession, I am forever grateful.

Preface

Scotland has more than its fair share of battlefields, and this patchwork of blood soaked landscapes stands as testament to this small nation's turbulent and often violent history. A few of these have entered the popular imagination, their names conjuring vivid images of victory and defeat, and fewer still, namely Bannockburn and Culloden, have been commemorated by visitor centres and display boards. But the same cannot be said for the vast majority of these sites of conflict, where thousands of men once faced one another in desperate life and death struggles.

The battle of Linlithgow Bridge (1526) is one of the forgotten, a battle which even as a battlefield archaeologist I was only vaguely aware, until that is I had the good fortune to encounter Jon Cooper, the author of this book.

We first met in 2003 at the annual re-enactment of the battle of Bannockburn in which Jon was participating as the commander of a schiltron of Scottish spearmen. Although I had fully intended to enjoy the day as a civilian spectator I was invited to take part, and so never one to turn down an opportunity to dress up I donned a tin hat, smelly leather jerkin and heavy gloves before enrolling with Jon's schiltron, where I had the pleasure of him shouting at me for the next hour or so as we clashed with our English foes. All good fun, and I suspect an experience bearing only the smallest resemblance to the bloody events of that September day in 1314.

That is not to say that the event had nothing to offer the historian eager to understand the experiences of the fighting man in battle, and these lessons have not been lost on Jon, who has used them to make this book just that little more evocative and indeed informative. For instance, it was a sunny day when we re-fought Bannockburn, as it probably was on the day of the real fight, and with the exertion and all that heavy gear, there was very soon a real danger of dehydration - which entailed everyone being well supplied with water by one of the camp followers. As a novice at these things it also drove home to me the importance of group cohesion, the slightest break in formation, caused by over-enthusiasm or lack of concentration and the game's a bogey; the enemy are in and the schiltron cut to pieces.

When the fighting was over and the English well and truly routed Jon and I got talking about his interest in the battle of Linlithgow Bridge, for which he had been a champion for some time. Several weeks later we met up in a pub at one end of the present bridge and discussed the possibility of carrying out an archaeological project on the site. This was later followed up with a visit to carry out some exploratory metal detector survey. It was November and the day ranks among the most uncomfortable fieldwork experiences I've ever had, and having worked on archaeological sites in Scotland for most of my career that's saying something. It was freezing and the rain was horizontal. With our hands almost frozen to our machines a colleague and myself were ready to leave within about an hour, especially as we'd found nothing but bits of scrap and the odd tractor part. Jon, however, was totally focused on the task and did not want to give up, such was his determination to find something related to the battle. In the end we got to go home, but Jon, over the next few weeks continued to scour the fields and as will become apparent in the book, it looks as though he has made some progress in recovering traces of the battle. Needless to say Jon fully recorded the location of his finds and is keen that they end up in a museum - the undisciplined metal detecting of battlefields and the removal of objects from them should be a cause of real concern to archaeologists and anyone else interested in these important sites.

The archaeological potential of the battlefield notwithstanding, it was obvious from the start that that Jon had done a lot of research into this little known, but none the less important battle, and we talked briefly about the possibility of turning that work into a book. Well here is the result, and what a worthwhile effort it has turned out to be. In these pages Jon provides a clear and entertaining account of the historical background to the battle, which for too long has languished in the shadow of the great clash at Flodden, where thirteen years earlier the scene for Linlithgow Bridge was set by the untimely death of James IV.

This book encapsulates the whole story, from the background of broken alliances, political scheming and double dealing, family feuds and score settling, right up to what it may have been like for the individual fighting man wedged into the dreadful press of battle. Perhaps most importantly this book, through the use of historical accounts and an analysis of how the armies operated, places the battle within the landscape across which it was fought.

Archaeological work by myself and others has shown that these sites have much to tell us about historic battles and the times in which they were fought, it remains to be seen how many of them will still be there to be appreciated in the years to come. The preservation of battlefields as historic sites has become a heated subject in archaeological and heritage management circles, many of them having been lost under motorways, housing schemes, industrial estates or other manifestations of the modern world. Scotland lags behind England in moving toward the protection of these sites, to the extent that we do not even have a gazetteer of all the battle sites that may be under threat. This situation is however improving, with Historic Scotland, the body responsible for the protection of our national heritage, now addressing Scottish battlefields as a real issue. By putting the battle of Linlithgow Bridge back on the map this book will help to ensure that the lessons of the past are not lost on the generations of the future.

Dr. Tony Pollard
University of Glasgow
August 2005

Introduction
"A Body Rent to Pieces"

By midday on 4th September 1526, George Douglas had had enough. He grabbed the bridle on the horse and pulled it, and the youth who rode upon it, towards the sound of the artillery booming in the distance.

'Sire, rather than our enemies take you from us, we will lay hold on your body, and, if it be rent to pieces we will be sure to take one part of it.'

This was no normal teenage tantrum. For this was a matter of life and death to George. His brother was leading his family retainers against an army twice its number. Battle had been joined and the fate of Scotland's monarchy hung in the balance. That youth, who had been late out of bed, who had refused to muster the relief forces and who now feigned sickness to hold up the advance, was the key to the victory. His appearance on the field of battle would be as decisive as the arrival of the 3,000 reinforcements from Edinburgh and Leith he was leading. For every Scot would think twice before bearing arms against their King

13 years since the death of his father he had been raised by the rival factions in the Scottish lairds. Separated from his mother, imprisoned by his stepfather and abandoned by his uncle Henry in England, this was James's best chance of escape and to claim the throne for himself. His favoured uncle, the Earl of Lennox was ahead with 10,000 followers committed to his escape, if he could only delay the progress of the reinforcements surely the day would be theirs. He would be in Stirling with his mother Margaret, the Queen Dowager, by nightfall.

As the guns roared out across the river Avon, some 16,000 Scots faced each other in battle, both sides believing they fought for God, Scotland and their King. By the evening, the great hall at the Palace would be ringing with the sounds of partying as the victors remembered the events of the day and blessed their survival. 3,000 would be killed or maimed. The fields around the bridge at Linlithgow would be running red, the nunnery at Manuel would be crammed with the dead and dying, the bloated corpses would be seen floating into the Forth. Men would have run themselves to death or were hewn down by pursuing horsemen.

What had happened in the last 13 years, in the childhood of that boy King. The sons and brothers of those Scots that had fought and died side by side against the English at Flodden, now faced each other in a bitter conflict in the heart of their nation. At stake was no less than the throne of Scotland; to lose would mean tried for treason, lands confiscated, families exiled, and execution.

This is the story of that remarkable childhood, the warfare that dominated the period and the events of that day. This is the story of a forgotten battle marked only by crossed swords on a map and a pile of stones at the entrance to a housing estate. This is the story of the Heart and the Rose.

Robert Fleming's The Burgh of Linlithgow Quin - centenary Ode

She harks the shouts of feudal strife
And sees the Life's blood freely flow
As man against man warr'd to the knife
In days five hundred years ago.

Chapter 1
'Warr'd to the Knife'
Aftermath of Flodden

On the morning of 10th September 1513 the victorious English soldiers awoke amongst the dead on Branxton hill. Around them lay the bodies of over 7,000 Scots, amongst them was their King, James IV. Further up the hill surrounded by many of their kin folk lay the bodies of the Earls of Lennox and Argyll. They were counted amongst the nine earls, fourteen lords of parliament and seventy nine gentry who were lost that day. The majority of the ruling class of Scotland lay awaiting burial. All the main routes from the border to Edinburgh were filled with over 20,000 frightened fugitives announcing the great defeat. The people of Edinburgh panicked. The council ordered the streets to remain empty of wailing woman and suggested they go to the kirks to pray for the safe return of their King. They then made plans to build a wall around the unprotected part of the city[1] and prepare for the inevitable English onslaught.

Queen Margaret heard news of the defeat in her apartments at Linlithgow Palace. The persistent rain, which had bogged down the Scottish troops, now heightened the sense of depression. Her worst fears realised she faced an uncertain future. She felt no shock or remorse as she had predicted her husband's death some months before. She had shed her tears in the days leading up to the invasion and now she was strong and ready to act. She was 23 years old at the time of his death, a relatively mature age to take on the role of her husband and her foresight had at least given her time to plan for such an eventuality. Her first action was to move to a safer sanctuary and although she loved Linlithgow dearly it was too near the English. She arranged for her belongings to be loaded into carts and then before they were ready to go, she rode to Stirling. With her was her 17month old son James, soon to be crowned James V.

She wasted no time in calling together the remains of the Scottish council on the 19th September, declared herself the King's lawful guardian in accordance with her husband's wishes and set the date for James's coronation for the 21st September in the Chapel Royal in Stirling. She also called for a general council to arrange for the defence of the country and by 26th November they met again to invite John Stuart[2], Duke of Albany, son of James III's younger brother and convicted traitor, to be Governor of Scotland in the King's minority. Messengers were immediately sent to France to recall Albany.

Perhaps of greater importance, the Council agreed to continue hostilities with England despite the offers of a truce from Margaret's sister in law, Catherine, acting as Regent whilst her husband, Henry VIII, was fighting his own war in France. Lord Home was appointed custodian of the borders with the remit to bring law and order to the land and Lord Fleming sent to France as ambassador in order to raise more troops and funds. Troops were mobilised again and garrisons in all the major strongholds strengthened.

However, Albany never showed and the promised French help never materialised. By February of 1514 Margaret appealed to her brother for peace, a move that the war mongering Scottish nobles disapproved of. Here was an English Queen negotiating the surrender of the Scottish crown to her own brother. Despite her best intentions, Margaret was dividing her support between Pro English doves and Francophile hawks. By 1514 the rifts that were to plague the country for the next 14 years were clearly evident.

But the English support never materialised either. Henry VIII had been engaged in futile pursuit of glory in France throughout the Flodden campaign. He had led his army to Therouanne and Tournay and fought a glorious but altogether meaningless encounter at Guinegate, which came to be known as the Battle of the Spurs in referene to the enthusiastic pursuit by the English knights. Henry seemed altogether unimpressed when the news of

The return from Flodden A Victorian depiction of the return of the Scots to Edinburgh. The despair and shock are well conveyed but the clothing and armour are totally inaccurate.

Flodden reached him. Despite securing his northern border, the planned campaign in France of 1514 came to nothing and in March of the same year his great ally in Europe, the Holy League, collapsed. Without this promise of soldiers and money Henry was forced to sue for peace. Treaties were signed with Louis XII of France in the August and bound by the marriage of Henry's daughter Mary to the ageing King.

Henry however did declare himself the rightful guardian of James and called upon Lord Dacre, hero of the hour at Flodden and the governor of the borders, not to antagonise the Scots in any way. Henry hoped that this would persuade the Scots not to remove the King to a safer place and in effect deny him ready access should the need arise. But Dacre had other ideas and planned a winter campaign against the Scots at Jedburgh.

Now more than ever Scotland needed help from France but the new peace left them on the sidelines. Not only did Louis negotiate on behalf of the Scots without their presence but he also agreed to terminate Scottish raids across the border. This was a complete betrayal of the Auld Alliance. It seemed that the lives of thousands of Scots had been wasted at Flodden

Queen Margaret by Jean Perreal dated 1520
Queen Margaret was 23 when she was widowed. Her beauty and wit alone made her a very attractive prospective bride. But when it came to husbands her heart tended to rule her head. (Reproduced by kind permission of Scottish National Portrait Gallery.)

and never again would Scotland look towards France without trepidation and suspicion. Henry even arranged for Albany to be kept in France. Leaderless, without arms and finance Scotland was left to fend for itself.

To make matters worse Margaret had taken to her bed, not through illness but to give birth to Alexander - Duke of Ross, her dead husband's son. In her absence the Parliament decreed that the control of the Scottish fortresses was to become their responsibility rather than the monarch's and set about arming the garrisons. This was a flagrant attempt by the hawks to wrest control from the infirmed queen. Margaret was learning fast that she was no King, burdened by matriarchal duties and unable to assert the royal presence in the borders of her kingdom in the manner of her husband. Despite her popularity among the common people she was losing her grip on the country. Even her tenants now refused to pay their rent. However she did have one trump card to play; she had the power to choose her next husband.

Archibald Douglas the 6th Earl of Angus was the first to act to fill the role of suitor. In August, not even before the ink was dry on the Anglo - French treaty he wooed and married Queen Margaret.

Angus was an eligible bachelor, medium height and build, reddish hair and piercing dark eyes. He sported a closely trimmed beard and hard set features, which asserted a sense of aggression and ruthlessness. He was a great sportsman, keen hunter and renowned courtier. He too had lost his father and uncle at Flodden. Indeed he would be a fitting father figure for the boys.

KING·JAMES·5
NAT·1512·OB·1542

The Young James V The young James was the only child of four in his family to reach adulthood. He was born on Easter Saturday on 10th April 1512. His father died at Flodden when he was 17 months old. He spent his childhood under the care of his mother's suitors. By the age of 14 had witnessed his first battle. By the time he was 16 he had escaped from his captors and declared himself king' (Reproduced by kind permission of the patrons of the National Galleries of Scotland'

Both had more than romance in mind in the union. Margaret was grasping at the opportunity to raise her profile and since the death of his grandfather, Archibald 'Bell the Cat' Douglas, this Archibald was now Earl of Angus, head of the most powerful family in Scotland, the Red Douglases. This liaison would bring Margaret the money, troops and perhaps most importantly, the blessing of Henry her brother.

Angus however realised that those who had regular access to the King would ultimately control the country. What better way to seize the initiative than to assume the role of stepfather to the King of Scotland and brother in law to King of England. They were married secretly at Kinnoul near Perth on 6th August 1514.

Not all was going well for the pro-anglo newly weds. News came from the borders that Lord Home had succeeded in beating off the ill conceived raid by Lord Dacre at Belling Hill and was now launching retaliatory strikes himself. So successful was this campaign that Dacre fell from grace with his English paymasters. But Margaret needed a strong pro English faction in the country to support her and Home's actions were seriously threatening her power base. In court those Lords disgruntled over the choice of Margaret's husband and bitter about not being invited to the wedding, plotted to return Albany. Margaret once again called upon her brother Henry to send troops north to booster her flagging support but Henry refused her aid. He did however persuade the French to retain Albany. But the pendulum of power was about to swing again in the continent

In January 1515, Louis XII died and Francis I became the new King of France. Despite his young age (20 at the time of his coronation) he was a very astute monarch and immediately brought pressure on Henry by releasing Albany. In May Albany, escorted by a French and Scottish fleet, arrived off Dumbarton. But it was a measured response, as Albany did not return with the arms and equipment the Francophile Scots longed for, but instead he invited them to renegotiate the peace so rudely broken by Home's raids. The council had no other option but to agree and a new treaty was signed. This time around the pro French faction was content with the new terms. It appeared the ghost of Flodden had finally been appeased.

By July Albany had won over the Lords and the parliament confirmed him as Regent. Even Angus agreed to support him, much to Margaret's disbelief. Disbelief turned to dismay when the parliament declared Margaret's stint as the King's guardian was over. She was to choose four out of eight candidates, nominated by them, to be the new guardians and allow the King to be taken to Edinburgh. Margaret refused and called upon her husband to protect her. Angus was forced to decide where his loyalties lay and in turn he retired to his fortress at Tantallon to let his wife deal with the issue. John Stewart 3rd Earl of Lennox and Gilbert Kennedy, 2nd Earl of Cassillis were sent to besiege Stirling and return the children to Edinburgh but Margaret, without her husband's support, bravely closed the gates on the besieging troops and sent word

The Royal Chapel in Stirling Castle The Royal Chapel in Stirling was the location of James's christening. (Authors Collection)

to Henry for help. None came and Margaret finally conceded to release the King to Albany's custodianship, notably getting James to hand the keys over to Albany in person. Albany was back and in charge.

Albany took to the task of governorship well, settling the borders and guiding the Scottish lords to some form of consensus. But he was constantly walking a political tightrope between the French backed lairds such as the Hamiltons and the Stewarts and the pro English Queen and her Douglas husband. The English looked upon his successes as a threat despite his adherence to the treaty and desperately tried to undermine his control through political intrigue. But the greatest problem Albany faced was striking a balance between Francis and his loyalty to James. So much so that he even threatened to break the ties altogether with France and look elsewhere for his Scottish allies. By 1516 his luck had run out and Albany found himself detained in France for almost 4 years. He had gone abroad to arrange the marriage of James into the French royal household and it was agreed under the Treaty of Rouen. But Francis and Henry were still on good enough terms for Francis to detain Albany at his pleasure.

In January 1518 Margaret found out about Angus's infidelities with his ex fiancée, Lady Jane Stewart of Tranquair. It was the last straw in their relationship and she severed all connection with him and his family. Instead she turned to James Hamilton the 1st Earl of Arran, sworn enemy to the Douglases and current Regent, for support. Arran acted fast in an attempt to deliver a knock out blow on the Douglases. He convened parliament and demanded that Angus attend to face accusations of treason. Angus refused to attend and to make matters worst, he seized Margaret's estates and in turn, the rent. Margaret found herself penniless again and looked to the Council to fund her court. But then Henry stepped in and, not wanting to see his sister dependent on the Scottish parliament, prevented her from going cap in hand. Margaret pleaded with her brother for help suggesting if she were to divorce, he could choose her next groom. Ironically, Henry was horrified at the thought of a divorce that was, in his eyes, totally immoral and demanded that she returned to her husband's side. Margaret had no other option but to obey and return to Edinburgh, a recently acquired Douglas stronghold. She was met by Angus who escorted her into the city, accompanied by a salvo from the castle artillery and the sound of pipes and drums. Two months later Angus had returned to his mistress in Tranquair and seized the Queen's remaining estates.

In 1519 the deadlock in Europe was to be broken by the emergence of Charles V, the grandson of Maximilian and now heir of the Holy Roman Empire. On Maximilian's death, Charles added the Empire to an already impressive real estate; Spain, Northern Italy and the Netherlands all came under his control. He was also reaping the benefits from the wealth and prosperity found in the New World. A more disturbing aspect to Francis was that the Empire now surrounded France. Henry immediately responded by forming an alliance with Charles in 1521 on what was to become known as the Field of the Cloth of Gold, so ornate was the pomp and ceremony.

Francis once again turned to Scotland for an ally and set about appeasing the council by releasing Albany and despatching with him instructions to prepare for a new war with England. But Albany returned to a very different Scotland to the one he had left. Angus held Margaret and the King in virtual captivity and the Douglases and Hamiltons had been at each other's throats since the previous year's debacle in the capital, commonly known as 'Cleanse the Causeway.

1 Now known as the Flodden Wall, traces of it still remain in the city
2 Albany was actually a 'Stewart, but he had spent all his life in France and therefore spelt his name in the French style of Stuart.

Chapter 2
'I shall fight today where you shall not be seen'
Cleanse the Causeway

In 1520 Arran had tried in vain to dissuade Margaret from returning to Angus and now took it upon himself to prevent Angus securing the King. He had ridden to Edinburgh at the head of 500 hundred armed men with the objective of seizing Angus. This was all to be under the pretence of calling a convention to talk over their differences. According to Robert Lindsay of Pitscottie in his history of the period, written in 1575, each man was:

'well accompanied and arrayed with jack and speir'[3]

Finding Angus in the city, Arran ordered the city gates to be locked but was dismayed to find that Angus also had 500 of his followers at hand.[4] With the tension mounting the citizens prepared themselves for the inevitable confrontation. To make matters worse for Arran, the guildsmen of Edinburgh held a grudge against him since, as Provost, he had sided with the Leithians against them in a dispute about a recent arrival of a cargo of wood on a Dutch ship. They were soon to be given the opportunity to show their displeasure.

There followed a tense stand off as both sides looked to gain advantage and neither wanted to be seen as the instigator of violence. Arran's uncle, Gawain Douglas, Archbishop of Dunkeld was placed in the role of peacekeeper and negotiator mainly due to his pious and caring nature. He called upon Archbishop James Beaton, latterly a Hamilton supporter and great friend of Gawain, to remonstrate with his allies and as a fellow churchmen and official representative of the law, sue for a peaceful settlement. They met at Blackfriars Wynd to discuss a suitable course of action.

However Beaton had resigned himself to confrontation and met Douglas wearing a mail haulberk under his robes. He was at once quizzed by Douglas about the imminent debacle and declared 'upon my conscience I know nothing of this.' And as to show his honour he struck his breast with his fist causing the chainmail to rattle. Douglas, now aware that Beaton was armoured ready for the fight, sourly remarked 'My Lord your conscience clatters!'[5]

Clense The Causey This Victorian print shows type of fighting at the barricades along the High Street. However, once again the clothing and equipment is fanciful. Kilts and morions are a figment of the illustrator's imagination.

Realising both sides were set on a fight, Douglas found his nephew to warn of the Hamiltons' intent and then withdrew to his chapel to pray. Angus went on the offensive, arraying his supporters at the Netherbow gate. Many of the Hamiltons had taken to their lodgings and as they slept Angus had his men blockade the yetts and alleyways, hemming the residence in. Undoubtedly the vengeful guildsmen acted as 'agente provocateurs', ensuring the Hamiltons were kept duly occupied.

It was to fall upon Patrick Hamilton of Kingscavil, the fourth bastard child of Arran, to trigger the action. Patrick had won notoriety in a duel with a French mercenary, John Coupante, some years earlier in Edinburgh castle, in which despite being unhorsed he had ended up forcing the Frenchman to yield. Renowned for his hot temper and love of a good fight he was to be the spark in the powder keg.

Spurred on by Sir James Hamilton of Finnart to take action, Patrick declared 'I shall fight today where you shall not be seen'[6] and made his way onto the High Street in a furious rage accompanied by his friend the Maister of Montgomerie. They ran straight into Angus and in a fit of anger started a street brawl. The cries from the street alerted the sleeping Hamiltons who tumbled out after them in an attempted rescue but instead found themselves trapped in the side streets where they were set upon by the Douglas contingent.

George Buchanan, a contemporary chronicler writing in his Scottish history describes the action:

'immediately he [Angus] and his party, having buckled on their armour seized upon the broadest street in all the town. He had about fourscore in his train, but all stout and resolute men and of known valour. They divided and posted themselves in the most convenient places, and so set upon their enemies as they came out of several narrow alleys at once; first they slew, and drove the rest back headlong, tumbling one upon another in great confusion'[7]

The scene was horrific as in each road and alleyway men set about each other with bill and spear, sword and knife, the sound of harquebus fire resounding across the city. Douglas's men resorted to ransacking known Hamilton safe houses, setting them alight in an attempt to smoke out the poor unfortunates. In the panic and chaos it was virtually impossible to prove allegiance to either faction before being put to the sword. Many fled the city to escape the fighting, others battened down their doors and hoped to be spared.

Pitscottie reckoned over 300 Hamiltons were killed, Buchanan states 72, in the fighting that followed in the alleyways and streets all the way up what is now the Royal Mile. Arran and his son only made their escape by seizing a packhorse carrying coal in from Leith and fording the shallows of the Nor Loch. Beaton had sought sanctuary behind the high altar in Blackfriars but was betrayed and pulled out into the street by the mob. He was only saved from murder by the intervention of Gawain who declared it a sin to put a hand on a consecrated Bishop. Angus sent out trumpeters to issue an ultimatum to all remaining Hamilton supporters to leave the city and Buchanan notes that one body of over 800 horsemen took advantage of this offer and left the city in disgrace. By nightfall the Douglases had control of the city and the castle.

James and Margaret remained oblivious of the whole affair, the King playing in the grounds of the castle throughout the fighting. The locals christened the event the ' Clense the Calsey' most likely after the battle cry of the Douglas faction .

3   "The Historie and Cronicles Of Scotland - Vol 2" by Robert Lindsay of Pitscottie trans JG Mackay

4   Buchanan suggests that Angus starts the battle with less than a 100 men but is joined during the fight by his brother William with reinforcements - "The History of Scotland" - George Buchanan trans J Aikman

5   "The Historie and Cronicles Of Scotland - Vol 2" by Robert Lindsay of Pitscottie trans JG Mackay

6   The Historie and Cronicles Of Scotland - Vol 2" by Robert Lindsay of Pitscottie trans JG Mackay (Scottish Text Society 1899 - 1911)

7   "The History of Scotland" - George Buchanan trans J Aikman (Glasgow and Edinburgh 1827 - 29) vol ii

Chapter 3
'Come Hame to Scotland'
Albany's Second Return

The Lords who met Albany, on 18th November 1521, did so with some trepidation. Many welcomed the return of the rightful governor and hoped for the repression of the Douglases. Others saw his onslaught against them and his apparent appeasement of Margaret as a sign of perhaps a more intimate relationship with the Queen dowager. Albany was undeterred and set to his task with vigour. He called a parliament and demanded the Douglases and their allies, the Homes, attend to face charges of treason. Angus was exiled to France and many of his followers fled to England. Albany confiscated their lands and returned the revenue to the Queen.

But when Albany attempted to raise the Scottish army for another invasion of England in accordance with his agreement with Francis, his support drifted away especially as there was no material backing from abroad. The Lords remembered too well the result of the last act of support for France and they were not prepared to put what little power they had on the line for another Flodden. Albany, desperate to unite the Scots again, appealed to Francis for men and equipment. And yet again events in Europe denied Albany his French troops.

Henry cited the release of Albany to return to Scotland as one of the reasons to renew hostilities with France. This time Henry decided not to go in person and sent over the Dukes of Suffolk and Surrey with a pitifully undermanned army. But it was enough to persuade Francis that there were no men spare to send to Scotland. Surrey could not repeat the victory of Flodden, limiting his action to minor skirmishes in Picardy and Artois, ending in a botched attack on Hesdin. Henry was keeping many of his best troops to deploy against a Scottish invasion and it was this that probably unnerved the Scottish nobles. Albany however had to be seen to attempt an invasion in support of the French. He raised his standard at Roslin and marched his army westwards to the border. However as he prepared to cross, the Earls of Argyll, Arran, Huntly and Glencairn all withdrew their support, claiming they were not prepared to risk another Flodden. Without them the invasion was to be a non-starter and by October 1522 Albany had once again returned to France pleading for more men.

With the Scottish army disintegrating and a temporary truce agreed, Henry was able to release more troops to France. In 1523 Suffolk returned to France ahead of some 10,000 troops, not in itself enough men to seriously contemplate the taking of Paris, but they had been promised troops from the Netherlands and Charles's German mercenaries. However neither of these forces showed up in enough numbers and Suffolk was limited to the pointless siege of Boulogne and an autumn excursion into Picardy. By the winter of 1523 Suffolk was forced to disband the remains of his disease ridden army and return home.

With Albany gone, Margaret called upon her brother to sue for long term peace on very attractive terms. Not only would the English return Berwick to the Scots and offer Princess Mary as bride to James but they also proposed a six year peace plan. Tempted by the offer and spurred on by the Queen, the Government came to within a whisker of accepting, but the pro French lobby held the decision at bay long enough for Albany to return; this time with money, equipment and men. Many had sworn an oath of loyalty to Albany before he had left, not to mention the receipt of a handsome bribe to ensure their support in his absence. The money proved enough and Albany returned in the nick of time to prevent an English take over.

In the summer of 1523 a French contingent of some 500 men arrived in Leith. The force in itself was inconsequential but it was enough for Henry to break the peace negotiations and to launch Earl of Surrey⁸ north into the borders once again. In June, the English burnt Melrose and followed this with almost daily raids into the 'debateable lands' along the border. By September, Surrey had mustered nearly 10,000 men and headed for Jedburgh. However the garrison of Jedburgh, some 1600 men under the command of Dand Kerr of Ferniehurst, fought furiously, house by house, before being overwhelmed. The epic defence of Ferniehurst castle followed and was again an English victory but at great cost. The English had to fight their way through the woodlands surrounding the castle before dragging their guns into position. Then they engaged in an artillery duel with the castle's arsenal until finally it was silenced and the garrison admitted defeat. That following night the English horses were spooked, possibly by a reiver attack and many of them lost. The English conviction wavered and the advance petered out. Margaret was furious. She called upon Surrey to march north to Edinburgh and if nothing else, rescue her and the King from Albany's pro French regime.

8 *He was son of the Earl of Surrey who commanded the victorious English army at Flodden*

Chapter 4
'Cust Downis our Howis of Defenss'
Albany's Third Return

By the 24th September the 500 Frenchmen in Edinburgh were soon swollen to over 4000 professional soldiers, many armed with modern firearms, artillery and pike. Albany returned with them, along with Richard De La Pole, the supposed 'White Rose' and pretender to the Yorkist claim to the English throne. Albany hoped to use De La Pole not only for his experience as a commander of Landsknechts, but also to raise sympathetic support in Yorkshire.[9] This was a formidable and impressive hard core of troops, something by which the Scottish lords could commit to. Albany also brought with him French gold, enough to catch the attention of the wavering lords. The pomp and ceremony of the march across to the capital was pure showmanship to attract recruits to the colours. Albany displayed his foreign troops in Glasgow and raised Scottish fervour with rousing speeches calling for the revenge of Surrey's raid on Jedburgh

By 23rd October Queen Margaret's spies were informing the English that over 60,000 troops were mustered outside Edinburgh and preparing to head south. She begged to be taken south but Albany posted 12 Scottish Archers of the French King's own bodyguard as a reminder of where her loyalties should lie. The English reacted swiftly with Berwick being put onto a war footing despite being stricken with plague and the walls of the town being in poor repair. Norham Castle was also fortified. The Northumberland militia was mustered but could only raise 2500 men. The corn was gathered in and the bridges over the Tweed and Till were destroyed.

Letters were sent to the Scottish lords dissuading them from joining the cause and word sent south to the young men at the English court to prise them away from their dancing and gaming and come north to defend their country. Clifford, Latimer, Darcy and Scrope heeded the call and came north. Approximately 50,000 troops stood to arms. The Marquis of Dorset was despatched to Alnwick, Darcy to Bamborough and Surrey took his van to Belford. The Banner of St Cuthbert, last deployed at Flodden, again accompanied the marching troops up to the disputed land of the borders.

But once again reaction in France and the problems of sustaining such a large army in the field spurred Albany on to committing his troops in a poorly planned campaign, in this case starting too late in the season against the well defended objective of Wark Castle. This time Lennox and Huntly, recipients of the letters from Surrey, attempted to withdraw their support on the grounds of poor recruitment, but Albany was not deterred. At the end of October 1523 he headed south along almost impassable roads and in atrocious weather, moving from Boroughmuir to Melrose and onto Eccles. By the time he reached the border his force was fading away fast and he needed a victory to hold the waverers in the ranks. He despatched 3000 men, mainly the French contingent with much of his ordnance to Wark, with the aim of securing the ford and capturing the castle whilst he took up residence in Home Castle.

9 *Nothing was to come of De La Pole's presence and he was to return to Europe only to die leading his beloved mercenaries at Pavia in 1525*

Chapter 5
'To be Murthered with Gunnes'
The Assault on Wark Castle

Wark Castle sits on the south bank of the river Tweed overlooking the associated village. It was originally a 'motte and bailie' design built by Walter Espec in the 12th Century and then going under the name of Carham. It became the centre of the cross border struggles, protecting the key fords along the Tweed. It was besieged in 1126, 1138 and 1139 leading to its rebuild in 1157. However all this work was in vain as again Wark was burnt by the Scots in 1399. In 1513 prior to Flodden, James had systematically bombarded Wark into submission along with Norham, Etal and Ford. After Flodden, Henry clearly viewed the position as a key point and commissioned Lord Dacre to redesign the castle in line with the latest defences against modern artillery.

The keep was designed to an unusual six sided plan, five storeys high and as the Duke of Norfolk described:

'in each of which there were five great murder holes, shot with great vaults of stone except one stage which is timber, so great that bombards can be shot from each of them'.

The top floor was strong enough to withstand the use of artillery and the floors underneath housed the accommodation for over 40 troops. A series of trapdoors allowed for the raising of powder and ammunition from the stores in the basements. The main keep was circumvented by a curtain wall or 'Ring', some 7m broad flat hard standing and whose wall was broken by 12 'embrasures' capable of taking cannons. The 'Ring' was exited by means of a steep staircase leading to an inner ward. This in turn led to an outer ward, the walls of which lay along the bank of the Tweed. Two gatehouses in this outer defence allowed for the passage along a causeway parallel to the riverbank, which led up from a ford. The gatehouses were three storeys high with a porter's lodge in each and a vaulted entrance. The wards were designed as sanctuary for the local population and could hold up to 1000 horses. The improvements of 1517 also included stables, a bakehouse, kitchens and the constable's lodgings all in the inner ward. The castle was far from pretty but a great example of the new style of fortification springing up in the advent of gunpowder.[10]

The defence of the castle was entrusted to Sir William Lisle and some hundred men. He was effectively cut off from Surrey's reinforcements in Berwick and Alnwick by the poor roads and dreadful weather. But they were well supplied and adequately armed, and no doubt took some succour from the knowledge that the weather would hamper the Scots as much as it would them.

Albany's task force appeared on the Scottish bank of the Tweed on 29th October. They spent the Saturday through to the following Monday preparing for an assault and bombarding the outer defences. Lisle's men kept their heads down, conserving their ammunition and awaited the assault. News of the attack reached the Earl of Surrey on Holy Island on the Sunday

The River Tweed below Wark castle The River Tweed below Wark. The Scottish guns were lined up of the plain on the far side. Normally the river is fordable but in 1523 the river was swollen by winter rains and the French resorted to boating their men across for the assault on the castle. (Authors Collection)

evening and he immediately despatched messengers to the Earls Of Northumberland and Westmorland at St Cuthbert's and Lord Dacre based in Alnwick telling them to meet him at Barmoor Wood some five miles from Wark.

Whilst the Scottish artillerists kept up their bombardment, the French troops commandeered and made boats and rafts. The Tweed, although fordable at Wark for most parts of the year, was now in flood and the Scots were forced to undertake an amphibious assault. At around 3.00 pm on the Monday the 2000 Frenchman led the waterborne assault on the outer ward. Paddling furiously against the strong current and disembarking on the muddy foreshore, the assault teams scrabbled to the walls with ladders and powder charges. They assailed the outer ward and the fosse bray with little opposition and then threw themselves into the more stoutly defended inner ward. The Earl of Surrey takes up the account in a letter to Henry after the event:

'And by Sir William Lisle captain of the castle without with him were right manfully defended by the space of one hour and a half without suffering them to enter the inner ward but finally the said French men entered the inner ward which by the said Sir William and his company freely set upon them'[1]

Lisle was not the kind of man to give up without a fight, declaring:

' the more shall our honour be to dye in the fight , than to be murthered with gunnes '[2]

And with that he led the surviving defenders back into the inner ward. In a vicious hard fought fight the French, tired after the assault, hemmed in the confines of the ward and hampered by the smoke from the burning buildings in the outer ward, gave way and fled to the boats.

Leslie suggests the withdrawal was more down to the weather than the bravery of the defenders:

' the affault leffit quhill within the nycht that they wor constraint be mirkiness to retire thair in, prrpofeing the nixt day being the fird of Novemenber to hauf affenyeit the fame of new, bot thair wes that nycht fic are vehement storm of tempestuous woodar quhairby thay weir constrainit to leif thair interprise at that tyme and return thame to thair army left be the ryfeing of the watter of Tweid that mychit haif bere cutt if be thair enemies'[3]

The Scottish artillery may have been in a position to stem the flight but they had got word of Surrey's rendezvous at Barmoor Wood some five miles away and his imminent arrival with over 5000 horsemen.[14] By the time the French retreated the Scottish artillery had already harnessed their oxen and were hauling their guns back to Albany's main army in Eccles. At 12.30 on the Tuesday the army lost its nerve altogether and headed home.

Surrey arrived to find over 300 dead Frenchmen in and around the wards, but he was unable to pursue Albany's men, shielded as they were by border horsemen. Furthermore, his force was in no fit state to pursue in such foul weather conditions, lacking supplies, and more importantly, wages.

Surrey's letter goes on to plead for more money to keep his army together offering to pay some of the wages himself before the King's money should arrive:

> *'And if the army should be discharged tomorrow next I think 10,000 marks will not pay that is owing and conduit money home.'*[15]

Instead of pursuit Surrey had his men reinforce the broken defences of the castle with earthworks and temporary defences. Certainly Wark had survived yet another turbulent assault but it had the scars to prove it.

But Surrey had little cause to worry. Albany's army was in a very much worse state. The French had lost all credibility despite their gallant assault and heavy casualties. The Scottish lairds had had enough, and remembering how they had been let down by the French advisors at Flodden, now marched their men away. A force of nearly 40,000 survivors disintegrated into a rabble for the retreat north as the winter's snow covered their tracks. The French were placed on ships and sent home, 500 being ship wrecked on the Western Isles in the winter storms, where those not murdered by the locals starved to death.

10 *For a wonderful virtual tour of Wark visit the Past Perfect website at www.pastperfect.info: the virtual archaeology of Durham and Northumberland*

11 *Letters and Papers , Foreign and Domestic of the reign of Henry VIII (Vaduz, 1965.)*

12 *Letters and Papers , Foreign and Domestic of the reign of Henry VIII (Vaduz, 1965.)*

13 *The Historie Of Scotland - Vol 2" by Jhone Leslie Ed Thomas Thomson (Bannatyne Club 1830)*

14 *Buchanan who was serving in the Scottish army at the time suggests that ' the English were coming against them with a numerous army, their own writers say, no less than 40,000 fighting men' This suggests the Scots greatly overestimated the relieving force. "The History of Scotland" - by George Buchanan trans J Aikman (Glasgow and Edinburgh 1827 - 29) vol ii*

15 *Letters and Papers , Foreign and Domestic of the reign of Henry VIII (Vaduz, 1965.)*

Wark Castle The grass covered base of the keep and remnants of the curtain wall is all that is left of Wark's defences. In 1523 English defenders rained down fire on the unfortunate French, and then sortied out to repel their attackers in a hand to hand melee. (Authors Collection)

Chapter 6
'Will not leave the King for danger'
The First 'Battle' of Linlithgow

The whole adventure had been a costly and demoralising affair. The collapse of the Scottish French army after Wark was the last straw for Albany. He once again made his way to France on the promise of returning in the spring with new resources. But this time he never returned. Albany had suffered from the after effects of Flodden. The Scots, drained of confidence, sceptical of the Auld Alliance and plagued by in-fighting had consistently failed to back him. Despite this he had kept a free Scotland for his King and never once had he prejudiced his loyalty.

With Albany gone for good, Henry thought he would have all his own way in Scotland. He was sadly mistaken as Margaret took full advantage of her proximity to the King and called upon Arran as her ally. Arran, still smarting after Cleanse the Causeway and now supported in some part by English bribes was happy to help especially as the Duchess of Albany had just died leaving no surviving children. He felt that this was the only way he would have a say in the naming of the future king. Their plan was simple. James now twelve years old, was to be taken to Edinburgh and adorned with the symbols of sovereignty. On the 26th July 1524 James escaped from his French captors at Stirling and rode for the capital. By the end of the same day his minority was declared over. Of course the real decision makers were to be Margaret and Arran. On the 1st August the King called the first Privy Council meeting in which all the officers were asked to refute their oaths to Albany or face dismissal; the majority complied without question. It was a simple card to play but no less effective for it. A few supporters of Albany, objected to the move, most notably Archbishop Beaton. Margaret and Arran moved fast to imprison him. The rest of the opposition including Lennox, Moray and Argyll held their tongues in face of this aggressive reprisal.

Margaret however again alienated the Lords just as she had laid the foundations of her power. Harry Stewart, a captain of her guard and eight years her junior and son of the Lord of Avondale was seen around court much more, offering advice and support. He replaced the trusted Patrick Sinclair as messenger and took up residence in Holyrood with the Queen. It was all too much for many of the lords and there was still the matter of her second husband. Angus was back in England and with the blessing of Henry was heading north to claim his matrimonial rights and seek reconciliation.

Margaret in the meanwhile sued for a divorce on the grounds that James IV was actually still alive after Flodden and had gone on a pilgrimage to the Holy Land. She had cleverly tapped into the common disbelief that such a popular King could not actualy have been slain. Many thought James to be a guardian of Scotland destined to return from Jerusalem, if not from the dead, in time of dire need. She left the details of the divorce to Albany, who willingly took up her cause in the hope it would undermine Henry's influence in Scottish affairs. Not only did he secure the divorce from the Pope, but he did so at great personal cost to himself. However it was finalised too late for Margaret.

But Angus was back with a vengeance. After being held up at the border by Dacre he moved swiftly to Edinburgh. He raised 400 men including those under Lennox and Scott of Buccleuch and smuggled them into the city. He then marched to St Giles and declared himself before the council demanding his rights as a husband. Margaret, awoken from her sleep, ordered the guns at the castle to fire on St Giles and set about raising her guard at Holyrood. As the two sides faced each other, the boom of cannon echoed down the mainstreet, and shot crashed into the houses around the cathedral. None of Angus's forces were hit but it was noted that two merchants, two priests and a woman were killed. Margaret fearing perhaps another Causeway bloodbath, lost her nerve, and ordered the guns to stop firing. An uneasy stand off followed but after four days Angus, having faced down the opposition, retired to Tantallon. But now he had the initiative and, calling upon his supporters to boycott the next Parliament called in Stirling, he asked to be returned to his place on the council. Margaret realised he had called her bluff and despite James wanting to march on Edinburgh wearing his father's sword and her nobles asking for him to lead the army against the Douglases, she seceded to Angus's demands to sit on the parliament.

In February 1525 Angus rode into Edinburgh with Lennox at his side along with a force of over 2000 men to take up his seat. This time his men were billeted well out of range of the castle's guns. On the 23rd he processed beside Arran and behind his wife and stepson as they opened parliament. Angus was back in power and about to play his trump card.

Angus' final bid for power took the form of a bloodless coup. He persuaded parliament to agree the setting up of a council of noblemen to look after the King for four months at a time.

He would naturally head the first group with Earl Of Morton, James Douglas and Gavin Dunbar, the Archbishop of Glasgow. Angus would then hand over to the second group headed by Arran and Hugh Montgomery, 1st Earl of Eglington. Cardinal Beaton and Argyll headed up the third and the final group consisted of Lennox, Montrose, Maxwell and Glencairn. Angus duly assumed the powers invested in him by the parliament but when it came to handing over the responsibility, he refused to do so. It was a master stroke of political gamesmanship which left a bitter taste in many of those deprived of their turn.

Arran in particular retired to Linlithgow to contemplate his next move and it was whilst at the palace that Margaret contacted him. She had moved north, away from her estranged husband's power base and had built up a friendship with Earl Of Moray. In January 1526 the Queen and Moray had accused Angus of treason and 'invassaling his prince to his attendance'. Now they were preparing to act on their accusations. Angus called upon his brother George to 'persuade' the King to write a letter stating that he was a willing guest of the Douglases. The King sent the letter but also smuggled out other correspondence refuting all that he had written and calling upon his mother to come and save him by force of arms if necessary. By the middle of the month the Queen and Moray were prepared to march south with some 600 followers in an attempt to wrest the King from the Douglases and requested Arran to side with them. They planned to join forces on the Linlithgow Peel before marching on to Edinburgh on the 10th January.

Hamilton Land The Hamilton Lands were built for the Hamiltons of Pardovan along the High Street in Linlithgow. They date back to the 16th Century and are typical of buildings that would have lined the High Street at the time of the battle.(Authors Collection)

Tantallon Castle   Fortress of the Douglases and their base in the turbulent period after the battle. Tantallon withstood the siege by James's avenging force in 1528.   (Authors Collection)

According to Douglas writing to Thomas Magnus the English ambassador, Hamilton was able to muster in the region of 5,000 men from the local estates around Linlithgow at the 'wappinschaw' including Lords Eglington, Cassilis, Sympill, Avandale, Ross and Hume and the Abbot of Jedworth and the Laird of Ferniehurst. They pitched camp around the Peel and awaited the arrival of the Queen's contingent. Angus seized the initiative, placed the King at the head of the Edinburgh militia and along with Lennox, Argyll and some 7000 troops, marched on the rebels on the 16th January. Arran had made no effort to construct a defensive position and with the royal banner approaching, he was easily dissuaded by the Lord Chancellor Beaton and the Bishop of Aberdeen, from taking up arms against the King on his own. His army returned to their houses and Arran fled. Douglas notes with some irony:

> 'war warnyt of oure cummyng and incontinent there ffir dislugit thareself, fled and left the toune, quhare we logit that nycht.'[16]

Arran met with Moray, the Bishop of Ross and Queen Margaret on the road to Stirling with 'sundrie uther northern men'. The Queen joined him in the flight to Hamilton whereas Moray rode on to Linlithgow and met with Douglas a mile out of town probably at the bridge. Realising all was lost Moray promptly threw in his lot with the Douglases, claiming he had been deceived by the Queen into believing the King was in need of rescue. The Douglases spent the night at Linlithgow Palace partying[17], safe in the knowledge that any man who bore arms against him was doing so against his King.

Angus was in complete mastery of the crown. When Beaton was asked by the King in another one of those 'letters' to hand over the Great Seal, he sent it, not to the King, but straight to Angus. This was a blatant acknowledgement by Beaton of where the real power now lay.

By March however the pressure was building on Douglas. On the 18th he wrote to Magnus again excusing himself from attending a Peace Day with Earl of Westmoreland because:

> ' Will not leave the King for danger' and 'all my lords have left except Glasgow and Lennox"[18]

Magnus replied stating that they, the English, would look towards Angus[19], Argyle and Lennox should Albany return to Scotland. However Magnus held some reservations of his own, writing to Wolseley on the 20th that the council had been :

> 'overshot for feigned reasons'[20]

In the meantime Margaret did her fading cause no good at all when in March she married Henry Stewart. This time her marriage was more for pleasure than for political gain but it so angered Arran that he defected to the Douglas cause taking with him many of his supporters that had gathered at Linlithgow that winter.

Angus went on to try to secure his power by having parliament declare in June 1526 that the King had officially reached his 'majority' and should take on full powers of his kingship. This cancelled out all other power sharing agreements and placed the King on the throne with Angus as his right hand man. From henceforth any attack on Angus would be seen as an attack on the King and an act of treason punishable by death. Angus then flooded the royal household with his family members often creating meaningless positions to do so. It meant that Douglas's men surrounded the King, day and night. Now more than ever James felt a prisoner to his stepfather.

Angus however had unwittingly sowed the seeds for his own downfall. James embraced his newfound authority and was in a position to take more risks. In June, a secret committee was set up within parliament to assist the king. Again Angus was among the instigators but amongst the members was the Earl of Lennox, uncle to the King and a firm friend. Lennox was young, dashing and well admired by the court. He to had lost his father at Flodden. Yet he was no supporter of lost causes, refusing to support Albany in his reckless excursions into England and had already ridden in support of Douglas on his return. Now he was to be called upon to

Kinneil House in Bo'ness Kinneil House was a Hamilton stronghold at the time of the battle. Hamilton's men mustered here before moving to Linlithgow. Much of the house post dates 1526, the structure to the right is the main dwelling at the time of the battle. (Authors Collection)

support his King. In an extraordinary act of independence, James chose Lennox 'fyrst and befor ony man' to be his advisor. This was a blatant rebuff of the Angus's domination. Lennox could not be considered an innocent bystander in these affairs, as his family were the next in line to the throne after the Hamiltons and before the Douglases. Lennox was orchestrating his own coup over the Hamiltons and whether or not he had a say in the king's pledge, he was more than happy to take on the role. Certainly his support of Douglas in the first bloodless confrontation at Linlithgow was in line with the Lennox strategy to usurp the Hamiltons.

Likewise, Angus's apparent unconditional acceptance of Arran despite the treasonable act at Linlithgow had left Lennox with no alternative but to swap allegiance to the Queen and he took with him Glencairn and the Earl of Cassillis. Lennox's first promise to his new ally was to plot for the King's safe return or die in the attempt.

Lennox got his first opportunity to fulfil his promise in July 1526. The pressure on Angus to address the mounting unlawfulness in the borders was growing since he had failed to attend the previous Peace days. The Armstrongs had mounted recent raids into England using the Nixon properties as safe houses. The council of Scotland wrote to the Earl of Cumberland acknowledging receipt of his complaints and reiterating their intention to destroy all the thieves. The letter ends by declaring that King James will leave Edinburgh on the 17th July for the Borders with the intent of punishing the thieves.

Angus arranged a Justice Ayres, an open court, in an attempt to bring law and order to the Borders and in order not to let the King out of his sight he took him with him. Lennox let slip the itinerary to Sir Walter Scott of Buccleuch, sworn enemy of the Kerrs and the Humes and therefore Arran. Buccleuch recognised a chance to snatch the King from his escort and win his favour, and ultimately eject his family's enemies from court. Accordingly, he gathered his kinfolk and set an ambush at Melrose.

16 *Letters and Papers , Foreign and Domestic of the reign of Henry VIII (Vaduz, 1965.)*

17 *Ferguson recounts that the Exchequer Rolls states that King actually drowned a horse in the Loch that night - Linlithgow Palace - History and Traditions' By Ferguson (Edinburgh & London, [1910] p.106*

18 *Letters and Papers , Foreign and Domestic of the reign of Henry VIII (Vaduz, 1965.) -1526 - Angus to Magnus - 18th March*

19 *Letters and Papers , Foreign and Domestic of the reign of Henry VIII (Vaduz, 1965.) -1526 - Angus to Magnus - 18th March*

20 *Letters and Papers , Foreign and Domestic of the reign of Henry VIII (Vaduz, 1965.) -1526 - Angus to Magnus - 18th March*

Chapter 7
'Stoutlie Fordwart'
The Battle of Melrose

The Battle of Melrose is perhaps best known for its inspirational verse rather than its strategic importance as the descendent of the main rebel leader ensured the event was well documented within his own fictional work. Sir Walter Scott in his prose Ride to Melrose alludes to the fight in the verse:

> *When first the Scott and Carr were foes*
> *When Royal James beheld the fray*
> *Prize to the victor of the day:*
> *When Home and Douglas in the van*
> *Bore down on Buccleuch's retiring clan*
> *Till gallant Cessford's heart-blood dear*
> *Reek'd on dark Elliot's border spear*

Both Leslie and Pitscottie briefly describe the action but give little away as to the disposition of the forces. We are told that Buccleuch mustered some 600 - 1000 men[21] to his cause mainly from his own household but also from the other local families.[22]

Many were considered by Leslie as:

'thevies and broken men of the bourdoriss'[23]

and Pitscottie describes as:

'theiffis of Annerdill' and 'Liddisdaill'[24]

These men were more like the Border Reivers (so dear to Sir Walter Scott's heart); heavily armed light horsemen on cobs and nags more used to lightning raids and nightly excursions than stand up battles.

The King however was escorted by a more professional band of retinue troops and garrison from Edinburgh. He was accompanied by many of the lairds from court and family members of the Kerrs and Humes. His escort included Angus, George Douglas, Lord Fleming as well as Maxwell, Lennox, Lord Erskine and Niniane Creychton from Sanquhar. Lord Home and the Earls of Cessford and Kerr of Ferniehurst had taken their leave of the King to return to their homes but on hearing news of the plot they raised some 400 horsemen and went to assist Angus.

The exact position of the battlefield is difficult to establish. There are a number of local place names that do allude to the fight. Charge Law is reportedly the ground on which Buccleuch drew up his men before the attack, Skirmish Hill the site of the main action and Turnagain, a small eminence where the rebels rallied during the retreat. Certainly the King's forces were making their way from Jedburgh back up to Edinburgh when the encounter occured. They became aware of Buccleuch's presence before they had crossed the bridge as the reivers came:

'stoutlie fordwart in the backsyde of Hallidoun Hill'[25]

The King was hastened to Darnock Tower and left under the protection of George Douglas, now accustomed to the role of bodyguard and not surprisingly Lennox, happy to play no part in the affair and on hand to snatch the King away should the opportunity arise. The King is said to have watched the fight from the roof of the tower, which suggests the majority of the fighting took place on Darnock Green and affirms the naming of Skirmish Hill, the present site of the Waverley Hotel.

Angus gathered together the rest of the King's escort and if Pitscottie is to believed delivered a grand eulogy:

> 'Schir, zone is Ballcleuch and theiffs of Annerdaill witht him wnbessett your grace from the gait. Bot I vow to god, schir the sall ether fight or flie and he shall tairrie heir on this know and my brother George witht you witht ony wther companie thou pleis, and I sall pase and put zone theiffis of the ground and red gait into your grace or ellis die for it'[26]

And with that Angus dismounted from his horse and charged into the fray. The fighting was said to be hard with victory uncertain until Home showed up with the reinforcements.

> 'Bot at last Lord Home heirand the wordis of that matter how it stude returnit againe to the king in possibill haist witht him the lairs of Cessfurde and Fairniehirst to the number of iiijxx speiris and sett on fercelie wpoun the lape and winge of the laird Baccleucheis field and shortlie bure him bakvart into the ground.'[27]

Buccleuch was wounded and his men broke and fled west along the Tweed closely pursued by Ferniehurst and Cessford. The pursuit was so vigorous that the pursuers appeared to become isolated from their main body and Cessford was surrounded[28] and slain by members of the Elliot family and servants of Buccleuch.[29]

Casualty figures differ with Pitscottie suggesting at most over 400 men were killed from both sides. Certainly he states that the King was to have appeared 'heavie, sad and dolorous'[30] at the extent of the of the bloodshed. Angus returned in triumph and took the King into Melrose to celebrate his victory before returning to Edinburgh the following day.

The relief on the Scott Monument This relief on Sir Walter Scott monument on the Royal Mile depicts the actions that so inspired his work. Here a billman takes on a mounted man at arms. The study is as romantic as the poetry. (Authors Collection)

Angus found Lennox's reluctance to join him in battle somewhat disturbing. He began questioning his loyalty and rightly so. Lennox realised the time was now upon him to make his move. He left court assuring the King that he would return to rescue him or die in the process. He rode hard for the sanctuary of Stirling where, once safe within its walls, he called for a muster of the loyal men of Scotland. By his side appeared the Queen and Beaton along with Glencairn, Moray, Argyll, Bishops of Dunblane and Orkney, Crawford, Cassilis, Lords Lindsay, Ross, Semple, Lyle and Avondale.[31]

In August 1526 Lennox launched a daring pre-emptive strike of his own. Heading up some 200 horsemen he made to the Boroughmuir outside Edinburgh and there despatched a snatch squad of eight men and eight spare horses into the city. In the dead of night they clattered down the High street making for Holyrood. The King was pre-warned of the plan by the Master of Glencairn and both made for the rendezvous at the palace. However the plot was discovered and the horsemen intercepted. Glencairn fled and the King was moved to the house of the Archbishop of St Andrews where George Douglas and William Douglas, Abbott of Holyrood, with some 40 armed townsmen watched him nightly.[32]

Lennox returned empty handed from this raid and committed himself and the Queen's followers to one final military expedition. This was to be the third rescue attempt in the space of the year, and it was to be by far the bloodiest.

21 *Angus writing to Henry on 16th September suggests 3000 men arrayed against him and he had no more than 300 - Letters and Papers , Foreign and Domestic of the reign of Henry VIII (Vaduz, 1965.)*

22 *The Buccleuch Muniments details the remission against Sir Walter Scott of Branxholme, Sir John Granston, William Turnball of Mynto and others for their mustering their retainers at Melrose and Linlithgow. This includes the names of James Hoppringill, Walter Scott of Syntoun, Robert Scot of Alanehauch, Robert Scot of Hourpaslot, William Scot of Hassindene, John Scot of Borthauch, Philip Scot of Eidschaw, Robert Turnball of Halrowl, Johne Scot of the Valis, Symond Scot of Fynnyk, Maister Mychaeil Scot and ilkane of thame.*

23 *The Historie Of Scotland - Vol 2" by Jhone Leslie Ed Thomas Thomson (Bannatyne Club 1830)*

24 *The Historie and Cronicles Of Scotland - Vol 2" by Robert Lindsay of Pitscottie trans JG Mackay (Scottish Text Society 1899 - 1911)*

25 *The Historie and Cronicles Of Scotland - Vol 2" by Robert Lindsay of Pitscottie trans JG Mackay (Scottish Text Society 1899 - 1911)*

26 *The Historie and Cronicles Of Scotland - Vol 2" by Robert Lindsay of Pitscottie trans JG Mackay (Scottish Text Society 1899 - 1911)*

27 *The Historie and Cronicles Of Scotland - Vol 2" by Robert Lindsay of Pitscottie trans JG Mackay (Scottish Text Society 1899 - 1911)*

28 *Local legend says that the standing stone at Kaeside Farm marks the place where Cessford was killed.*

29 *It was this event that sparked off a bloody feud between the Kerrs and the Scotts. Walter Scott was killed in revenge in 1552 in Edinburgh. There is a monument by St Giles in the Royal Mile dedicated to Sir Walter Scott the 11th Earl of Buccleuch. The friezes around the base of the monument are a fitting testament to these troubled times and give a good indication as to the clothing and warfare of the age.*

30 *The Historie and Cronicles Of Scotland - Vol 2" by Robert Lindsay of Pitscottie trans JG Mackay (Scottish Text Society 1899 - 1911)*

31 *This list of 'rebels' appears in Angus's letter to Henry VIII - P228 State Papers Henry VIII volume iv p456 and The Douglas Book No. 99 State and Official letters.*

32 *State papers of Henry VIII Vol iv p 455 -457*

Chapter 8
'With Fire Flame and Hideous noise'
Warfare in Renaissance Scotland

It is a matter of conjecture as to what the armies that fought that day would have looked like as we have no eyewitness account. The battle fell between a number of great engagements; Flodden in 1513, Solway Moss in 1542 and the battle of Pinkie in 1547. We can come up with a fair idea as to the dress and arms of the combatants through a process of interpolation.

The army that went to Flodden was the biggest yet mustered by a Scottish King. James IV was a very forward thinking monarch more in the mould of a European Renaissance prince than a traditional Scottish king and as such he embraced the new sciences and philosophies with great enthusiasm. His appreciation of the latest advances in warfare was no exception and he not only gathered an incredible force for the campaign but also endeavoured to train them in the latest arms. To do this he called upon military advisors from France, around 40 of them, to train his men in the latest weapon - the Pike.

The use of the pike was not a new concept; in fact the latest craze was started some 50 years earlier with the all-conquering armies from the cantons of Switzerland. However this apparent military revolution could be traced back further. In 1513, the Italian, Bartelemio d'Alviano had reformed the Venetian army 'All antica', that is to say in 'the manner of antiquity'. Surprisingly for an Italian this was not in the manner of the Romans but in the style of the ancient Greeks.

In particular the armies of Alexander the Great and the Macedonian phalanxes that had dominated the battlefields of ancient southern Europe. The basic square pike blocks became the favoured formation for the new Italian armies and more devastatingly, the Swiss. A Swiss pike block could consist of anything up to 4,000 men and would act as the medieval equivalent of a steamroller, the sheer weight of numbers pushing the front rank onwards through what ever stood in its way.

The pike itself was made of well-seasoned hardwood, ideally ash, cut to 1 ¼" diameter at the stock and in some cases tapering to 1" at the head to reduce the weight. Traditionally the Swiss carried anything up to 18 ft pikes but many were cut down to 14 ft for ease of use and transport. The pike head was up to 12" long made of steel and in the style of a leafed point or a square sectioned, needle pointed bodkin. The head of the pike was protected from dismemberment by fitting lengths of metal along the shaft, called 'langets'.

To carry them on the march over the shoulder was a tiring business; not only did they need strength to balance but they also tended to 'bounce' which caused great

Pikeman The author demonstrates the use of the pike. This one has been cut back to 17ft to make it easier to handle. (Authors Collection)

discomfort. Most pikemen carried their weapon over any distance 'at the trail'; by the head and dragging the stock behind them along the ground. On the march the Swiss carried their pike in bundles on carts. Most modern day re-enactors would be the first to agree that the pike is best carried on a roof rack rather than on the shoulder.

On its own the pike is an almost useless weapon, very difficult to manoeuvre and once an attacker is 'past the point' it becomes a useless, cumbersome length of wood and is best quickly discarded. When used 'en masse' however the weapon comes into its element. Its length means that three or possibly four ranks could offer protection to the front rank. The front man would carry the weapon from the waist, the second and third rank at chest height and the fourth above their head with the points pointing downwards. The other ranks held their pikes across their chest and would add to the press by pushing against the man in front. Standing shoulder to shoulder on the front rank, with a possible three other weapons protruding between you and your neighbour meant any attacker was faced with a dense wall of spear points. If you got past one point you would fall upon another three and be hemmed in by the shafts either side. This, plus the weight of another 15 ranks behind this wall, meant that the momentum was massive. Anybody stuck on the London tube at rush hour will appreciate the surge effect of a mass of people all moving in the same direction. If a man on the front rank fell for any reason then he would soon be trodden over by his colleagues and replaced by the next man. At Flodden it was noted the English arrows had little effect on the Scottish Pike block as the density of the shafts formed a veritable latticework through which the arrows rattled down.

The Swiss had won a string of impressive victories at the beginning of the 16th Century. None more so than Novara in June 1513 when the French under Louis de la Tremoille were surprised at camp and soundly defeated by three Swiss pike blocks. It is not difficult to believe that it could have been these surviving veterans who were now advising the Scots before Flodden.

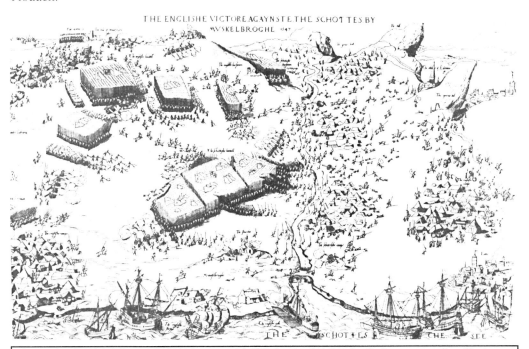

The Battle of Pinkie This contemporary portrayal of the battle of Pinkie clearly demonstrates the effectiveness of the combination of arms. The English employ pike, bow, shot, artillery and cavalry. The Scots in comparison field only guns and pike blocks. Their resulting flight is clearly illustrated to the right of the picture. (Reproduced by kind permission of the Edinburgh Central Public Library.)

But the Scottish pike both at Flodden and Pinkie were not Swiss and in both battles they failed to emulate their role models. Debatably, this could be put down to two main fundamental flaws.

The first is a matter of what the French would call 'elan'. The Swiss, like their Macedonian role models, had a great morale. Strict discipline and sense of Cantonal loyalty meant that every man in the pike block knew what to do and was prepared to do it. When a pike block went to battle, the chances of survival for the front ranks must have been very slim indeed. Surprisingly, it was considered an honour to volunteer for the front rank. In addition the German Landsknechts actually paid their front rank men double wages. However there was little dishonour in bringing up the rear and the fact that you were there at all was seen as worthy enough. It must also be noted that any man seen to run would be put to death by his colleagues there and then or at least after the fight was over.

The Scottish pike block was not as enthusiastic. Certainly the noblemen jostled and vied to be at the front to impress their King and peers. But the levies and 'pressed' men of the rear rank had little stomach for this new form of warfare. They were poorly trained in this new weapon and poorly armed otherwise. The chance to sneak away with all the leaders otherwise occupied in the front must have been very tempting. The fact that there were so many casualties at both Flodden and Pinkie could be put down to the fact that the rear ranks could not escape due to the impassable terrain to their rear (Branxton Hill at Flodden and the River Esk at Pinkie) and not for the want of trying. The Scottish pike block could be considered as having a tough outer shell but a soft centre.

Secondly, the Swiss, contrary to popular belief, used a combination of arms. Buzzing around the formation was a swarm of missile men. By the 1500s crossbowmen were making way for harquebusiers and gunners. These men would step out ahead of the pike block, sniping at range at the opposition, softening them up for the attack. Then as the pikes engaged they would drop to the flanks, protecting them from attack and getting around and behind the opposition. One in four of the Swiss force would have been a skirmisher. The Scots had nothing of the kind. The historical reticence to adopt the bow in any great strength had left the pike blocks at Flodden fatally exposed. At Pinkie, any Scottish 'shotte' was run down by the English cavalry and again leaving their unfortunate colleagues in the pike blocks to their fate. Without this combination of weapons a career as a Scottish pikeman was probably to be short lived.

The Scottish pike blocks at Pinkie are forced together in a similar manner to Lennox's men at Linlithgow. With momentum lost the back ranks begin to drift away. The front ranks take the majority of casualties with gaping holes appearing in the files. (Reproduced by kind permission of the Edinburgh Central Public Library.)

This close up of the Pinkie print show how the English effectively combined their arms. Horse artillery, pike and shot all supporting each other. (Reproduced by kind permission of the Edinburgh Central Public Library.)

It is reasonable to believe that there were pike formations at Linlithgow Bridge. The professional soldiers garrisoning the King's royal palaces and castles would probably have been armed with the latest weapons and equipment. They may not have had great faith in their own ability with the weapon but it would be conceivable that they mustered carrying their pike. The levy on the other hand would have been another matter. Many of the locals when called to arms would have reached for their grandfather's hand me downs or tools left around the farm or work place. When mustered they would have had little time to train or gain access to the town armouries. These men would have carried a mixture of weapons. So the massive pike formations of Flodden and Pinkie are unlikely to have been seen at Linlithgow. The bodies of troops here would probably have a hard core of pikemen and nobles in the front ranks backed up by the militias with their hotchpotch of arms grouping around their retinue banners and flags. It is doubtful that there would have been too much control of the ranks. Interestingly Pitscottie comments that when Andrew Wood found the Earl of Glencairn he was 'still fight and with 30 men left of all his army only unslain and fled from him '[13] infering that many did take to their heels and not much could be done to stop them.

Certainly, manoeuvring large bodies of untrained troops would have been difficult especially across difficult terrain. This was to be something that Lennox would have found out to his cost.

Polearms

The most common weapon used by the militias would have been the simple spear or half pike, a cut down version of the pike, anything from 6ft to 10ft long and like its taller counterpart protected by langets. The butt end may have been fitted with a point to drive into the ground to add steadiness to the weapon. The spearhead may have been fitted with lugs or 'boar stoppers' to prevent the point going too far into the target and not being able to be withdrawn.

However, the spear has only the thrust for delivering a fatal blow. In general polearms also combine the attack with a sweeping, scything motion of a blade and the delivering of a puncturing blow of a spike. The weapon may also provide a means of hooking the opponent knocking him off balance before delivering a more telling attack. Normally mounted on a 5-8ft hardwood shaft, such weapons as the bill and halberd had been derived from agricultural instruments used for scything hay or pruning hedges. It didn't take much imagination to see what effects such weapons would have on men.

For many years the Swiss had carried the halberd. Even by the 1500s with the pike as the predominant weapon they still saw the benefit of having a body of halberdiers to fall upon the unprotected flanks of the enemy's formations or as the final layer of protection for the standards or commanders. Flodden however had been a more fatal example of the devastation this weapon could have on a pike armed force. The English billmen had fallen on the disorganised ranks of the Scottish schiltrons with brutal efficiency, the King

The Billman The Author recreates the typical soldier of the Douglas Retinue. He wears a fixed sallet and almein breastplate as well as plate gauntlets. His coat is in the colours of his employer, the Douglas Family. Being an Englishman in Scottish pay he prefers the bill to the pike (Author's collection.)

himself hewed down by a 'noteable bill blow'. Once passed the point of the pike the Scots had to resort to their sidearms and these fell well short of the reach of the bill. Not to say it was an easy job, the consensus being that a man required four to five good strikes with a bill before a well-armoured knight would succumb to a fatal blow.

Even today a guard of Halberdiers escorts the Lord Mayor of London's coach and the 'soldiers' at the Linlithgow Marches carry halberds.

Other less frequently occurring polearms were war hammers, a weapon more suited to the nobleman from the Wars of the Roses some 40 years before. These two handed swinging weapons consisted of a hammer shaped head with a point on one side and crushing flattened head on the other. They may have also added a spike to add a thrusting element.

One weapon worth a mention due to a tenuous link with the Scottish armies of the period is the 'Leith' Axe. It is difficult to pin down the precise design of the weapon and its origins, suffice to say it was a polearm similar to a bill or Halberd with a double bladed axe head and similar to the French style[34] Why this design is particularly associated with Leith is a mystery and perhaps yet another Victorian myth, however Leith was a centre of the armouries trade with a number of craftsmen registered as Halberd makers. The constant presence of European mercenaries arriving in the port could conceivably have led to the demand for the weapon.

In comparison there are clear documents for the development of the Jedwart stave. This fearsome polearm consists of a four foot steel blade, a few centimetres wide, which protrude beyond the end of the shaft. The extension is double bladed and the shaft protected by 'rondels' that not only protect the hand but also add to its thrusting power. Strangely these weapons were withdrawn from use in 1515 by royal decree, presumably due to their inefficiency in any other hand than by a mounted border horseman. It could be claimed that they were simply too light to deliver a heavy telling blow. Despite this, they continued to appear in accounts up until the 1680s.

Certainly, the rank and file would have gathered to the colours with a wide assortment of weapons and farm implements, not all would have been well trained in their use but if carried in determined hands the weapons would have caused horrific injuries.

Swords, Bucklers and Sidearms
It is wrong to assume that the average man on the field would have been armed to the teeth with an array of weapons. Each man would carry a secondary weapon but this may have been more to satisfy the need for a multipurpose tool for living in the camp rather than for self-defence. Knives, hand axes and maules would have all been primarily for every day camp life but pressed into action as a last resort.

Knives were a functional tool and a status symbol. The most popular style were adorned with two lobes at the hilt and duly called kidney or bollock daggers. Quillons, metal pieces set perpendicularly into the base of the blade, were designed to protect the hand, but they were evolving into cages of metalwork, which by the 1570s were to become known as basket hilts. By the 1520s however the quillons were typically looping up at their ends in a manner designed to trap the attacker's blade and with a twist of the wrist, disarming him. Alternatively round plates or 'rondels' may have protected the hand. Blades ranged in length and cross section, but narrower, more pointed blades in the manner of the 'stilleto' were becoming more popular in an attempt to combine lightness and the ability to get into the chinks in the armour.

As blade lengths grew then the weapon became known as a basilard, a cross between sword and knife, these were very popular among the harquebusiers and archers. These were a cheap multipurpose tool and would not encumber the light troops with the burden of a full-length sword clattering around the calves.

A

B

C

D

E

F

F

CAPTIONS TO COLOUR SECTION

Cleanse the Causey   (by Alan Gault)

A1. This poor Hamilton retainer cowers behind his buckler awaiting his fate. He has been pitched out of his billet onto the streets of Edinburgh wearing little more than his shirt and hose. Only his cap badge identifies him as a Hamilton supporter.

A2. This armed Douglas man debates the fate of the assailant. He carries an older style sword and the fashionable rolled top breastplate over his linen shirt. Again his only form of identification is the 'Douglas Heart' cap badge and the colours of his hose

A3. This fully armed Douglas retainer wears a jack of plates over his padded jack and coat. He is about to deliver the fatal blow with his harlberd, trimmed down to allow for combat in the confines of the yetts and alleyways. He too carries a sword and buckler as secondary arms.

The French at Wark (by Alan Gault)

B1. The French took some 2-3000 men to Wark with Albany. They led the amphibious assault on the castle and left some 300 of their number dead in and about the inner ward. Their only reward for their valour was shipment back the France; 500 being lost in storms on the West coast of Scotland, the survivors of the wrecks either starving to death or being killed by the locals

The officer on the left supports the national livery of France for the period. Well armed and clothed he is well prepared for fight assault. He carries a fixed jawbone sallet under his left arm.

B2 The crossbowman on the right is also a professional soldier in French service. He carries a heavy crossbow and a quiver of 24 bolts. On his right hip he carries his 'cranequin', a rack and pinion system used for spanning the crossbow. He wears thick woollen stockings over his hose as added protection against the winter weather.

B3 The 'Archer' or Man at Arms in the background is of lesser noble blood hoping to make his name in the wars in Scotland He is heavily armoured and carries a bill. The cold Scottish weather is kept out by his cloak and thick woollen coat. All the figures depict the cross of St. Denis so as to identify their nationality.

The Hamiltons (by Alan Gault)

C1. The central figure shows James Hamilton, Earl of Arran making his way with his troops to the fighting on the morning of the battle. Fully adorned in his best livery, Arran wears a more dated suit of armour. His enclosed helm supports fashionable yet totally impractical ostrich feathers. His velvet skirt is adorned with the Hamilton cinquefoils

C2.The Hamilton retainer greeting his Douglas ally wears a simple jack, the rivots showing where the metal plates are attached within the lining. This armour is light, cheap and effective. He carries an. antiquated hand and a half sword. The man has brought a fearsome bill instead of a pike and would have fought around the standards in the Hamilton battle.

C3 The Douglas gunner is more lightly armoured, supporting an Almein breastplate and padded jack. His secondary armament is a roundel dagger. His gun is based on those seen on German woodcuts, he is also carrying his lighted match. His powder and shot are carried in a pouch on his belt.

The Lennox Men (by Alan Gault)

This scene depicts Lennox's men meeting the Cistercian mother superior at the Manuel Convent.

D1 The vanguard consisted of approximately 2000 light horse from the west coast. Lightly armed, these horsemen would have acted as reconnaissance for the Lennox advance. Here this horseman wears a simple padded jack and a plackart. He is armed

with a latch or light crossbow. This could be carried loaded but was difficult to reload once fired. They took heavy casualties in securing the ford and appear to cease as an effective fighting force soon after the crossing, either dismounting to join the main attack or pursuing refugees off the field

D2 The Master of Artillery has brought along a pioneer to translate. He is French and is obviously well paid for his position. He wears a mail shirt under his coat. The Lennox insignia is clearly displayed on his arm

D3 The Pioneer is wearing his normal civilian attire. Being a local he is happy to introduce the Frenchman to the sister.

D4 The Mother Superior is gesticulating towards the ford and doesn't seem too pleased to have her peaceful life disturbed by the army's presence. The crucifix is based on the one found on Manuel Hill during surveys of the battlefield.

The Highlanders (by Alan Gault)

E1. Lennox fielded over a thousand men from his estates in the Highlands. The central figure represents their chief adorned in the finest armour the 'Northmen' have to offer. Aketons were still the main form of armour but he wears leg armour and a chain coif more befitting his status.

E2 His 'Islesman' carries the fabled Claymore or two handed sword. This is based on an example in the National Museum of Scotland. These fearful weapons were well suited to lopping off the heads of pikes and pikemen alike.

E3 The Cateran has little or no armour. Bare legged with his tunic tucked into his belt all his has for protection is a half pike and skull cap. Contemporary illustrations of this type of garb could be mistaken as plaids. His possessions are carried in his haversack. He can only be fearful of his fate this day

The Turning Point of the Battle (by Alan Gault)

The Hamiltons surge down on the faltering Lennox troops. They have been joined by the Douglas reinforcements and realise the day is theirs. They renew the attack with bill and pike levelled at the heads of their enemy. The Hamilton banner flutters overhead. They step doggedly forward over the corpses of their colleagues. They have the momentum they have the advantage of ground and they know God is on their side

The Lennox retinue and highland men are in no condition to withstand this latest onslaught. With their lords and sergeants being skewered on the advancing pikes the lightly armed caterans begin to falter, push their way to the back, disrupting the formation and losing momentum. With cries of 'A Douglas ' ringing in their ears above the din of battle and the wailing of the wounded, the Lennox contingent breaks and runs. It's now every man for himself.

The Douglas Retainers (by Alan Gault)

G1 The central figure depicts Archibald Douglas reading the list of casualties after the battle. He wears a fine example of Almien armour under his coat. He has replaced his visored German sallet with a more comfortable velvet cap.

G2 He is accompanied by his standard bearer in similar attire, his coat removed to show the detail of the armour. He still wears his Italian sallet modelled on an actual helm in the Wallace collection. The standard is based on the Douglas banner now housed in the National Museum of Scotland.

G3 The drummer who has brought the lists to his lord is relatively well protected and shows a good combination of protection. He wears a mail shirt padded coat and 'coat of plates'; the many layers offering protection to different blows. His double hose are coloured in accordance to his retinue and emblazoned with the 'Douglas Heart' to ensure correct identification.

Swords, like knives, were a sign of distinction for an individual. Unlike 250 years earlier almost every man would be able to handle a blade to some effectiveness whereas before, swordsmanship was very much a sport of the nobleman. Most professional soldiers would carry a blade of some form, most likely a poor quality munition blade or 'hangar' supplied by the garrison armoury. Captains and noblemen were could afford to support a continental blade, again the grip being protected by the ever growing quillons and sometimes inscribed with family crests or encouraging slogans. Blades were beginning to get thinner and lighter as the full armour was making way for padded cloth or leather, a consequence of the introduction of the gun. Many, however would have carried their father's bulky 'hand and a half' swords and it would not be unknown for the weapons to date back some 50 years.

Use of the fabled 'Claymore' (or 'Great sword' as the translation would have it) is a subject of great debate. The awesome effect of a great man wielding such a two handed sword amongst the compact ranks of the pike blocks is a frightening concept.

The potential of such a weapon was not overlooked abroad. 5 1/2 ft long swords, some fluted or set with teeth, were already being used to chop into the forest of pike heads by the Landsknechts on the continent. These burly volunteers drawn by lot or prisoners in search of redemption formed the 'verlorene hoff' or forlorn hope, which marched ahead of the pikes in an attempt to engage with the enemy and causing as much disruption as they could before their colleagues hit home. Then, if they survived, they would fall on the flanks of the opposition and chop away at the unprotected sides of the poor unfortunates who could only hope their own 'flankers' would be at hand to help them.

The highland followers of Lennox would have brought with them similar two handed swords but it is less likely that they employed a similar tactic to their European counterparts. It must be remembered that wielding such a weapon requires great strength, stamina and space. The effectiveness of such a weapon in the press of men at the heart of the action must be reduced and perhaps such weapons remained more of a status symbol than a practical alternative to the lighter 'hand and a half' or short sword.

Shields

Unlike their Macedonian counterparts the Swiss pikemen did not carry shields. Likewise the Scots were reticent to be encumbered by them. However, the Scots nobility at Flodden were observed to carry pavises on their backs or by their squires. These large shields originated in the 13th Century in Pavia, Italy. They were often the height and the width of their owner and were designed to protect the exposed militia crossbowman whilst he was reloading. They were sometimes carried by a pavisier, initially a poorly armed assistant, but they developed into a well-armed spearmen capable of presenting the enemy with a mobile wall of spear and wood palisade from which the crossbowman could shoot. The French had taken the concept further during the 100 Years War by arming the front rank of their infantry with pavises purely to protect the men behind from the deadly English archery. They achieved a notable success in 1359 at Norgent Sur Seine where they defeated an English bow armed force.

The European pavise was made of laminated wood, curved around the owner covered in canvas or hide and often adorned with town colours or religious symbols. The pavises carried at Flodden were of a less subtle design but just as effective. Two laminated sheets were joined at an angle down the centreline of the shield. They were carried on the back until the wearer came to within missile range when they would be presented to the front. Whether the wearer could continue to advance holding the Pavise and the pike is debateable. It may have been more likely that the pike block halted to withstand the worst of the arrows before the front rank cast down the pavise and advanced on. Alternatively, the front ranks may have been able to shuffle forward weighed down by armour pike and shield. Whatever the drill, the English were dismayed to see their arrow storm come to nothing against this walking barrier of wood. There is however no evidence of pavises being used at Linlithgow or Pinkie. They were cumbersome and difficult to transport and needed a certain degree of training to be used correctly. However, it would not have been beyond the imagination of Arran to set up some form of barricade at the bridge or on Pace Hill and who knows, the odd veteran of Flodden may have set up the pavise to aid his defence.

The most likely form of shield would have been the target or buckler. These small round shields offered little protection against missile fire but were designed to parry weapon blows in hand to hand combat. Instead of hiding behind the static pavise or heater shields of the 14th Century, the buckler was used to parry blows with a counterpunch, almost like a steel boxing glove. Likewise, thrusting the boss or rim of a buckler into the face of an opponent could be a potent offensive counterblow. The armies of Europe made good use of 'sword and buckler' men, more mobile skilled swordsman moving around the battlefield like shock troops, often leading the assaults or screening advances. There is no evidence to believe that such a large body of men fought at Linlithgow but it would be the most natural use of lightly armed highlanders or the European mercenaries.

The target, perhaps better known as the 'targe' was of similar design and use as the buckler but tended to be made more of laminated wood covered in leather and of greater diameter. The ubiquitous studded targe is more of a 18th Century adaptation but gives a good indication of size and construction of the 16th century ancestor.

Bow

Much has been written about the War Bow and much surmised as to why the Scots failed to adopt it in any great measure despite being on the receiving end on numerous occasions. It is not the objective of this account to tread this well worn path. Suffice to say by 1526 it had been some 100 years since the heyday of the Scottish bow. In the 1420s the armies under the Douglases fighting in France had consisted of more archers than spear. So impressed was the Dauphin with their performance that he recruited a bodyguard of Scottish bowman. . However, by 1526 those days were long gone, the Scots had preferring to play football rather than practicing in the archery butts on a Sunday. The skills and training required to be a good bowman were on the wane. Even the English had started to replace their bowman with the new firearms. It is said that Flodden was the last 'bow and bill' battle fought by the English.

Not that the use of the bow was out of favour with the royalty. Henry VIII was a keen archer and James IV likewise would go hunting on the Riccarton Hills with the bow. Linlithgow Palace boasts a set of archery butts[35] and it is reasonable to think that the young James V would while away his captivity practicing the skill. They however would have never appeared on the field of battle so armed.

There were two groups of commoners who did still appear at the muster armed with the bow. The first were the Border horsemen who tended to carry as many arms as they could and used the short bow as a silent addition to their armoury. The second and more likely type of bowman appearing at Linlithgow were the Highland levy. It was noted at Pinkie that Huntly's division was flanked by a number of bowmen[36] acting as light troops but their contribution to the fight was limited as they were scattered by fire from the English ships off the coast. However despite its declining effectiveness, the bow was still carried into action as late as 1644 at the Battle of Tippemuir. It is safe to say that the Highland supporters of Lennox and Douglas would have likely headed to Linlithgow carrying bows.

The Bow or War bow (so as to distinguish it from the crossbow) would have been anything up to the height of a man, in fact actually one 'fitsmele'[37] taller than that according to

The old and the new discuss the merits of their chosen weapons. The Gaddgedlar re-enactors recreate the uniforms of the period and demonstrate both archery and gunnery techniques. (Authors Collection)

contemporary statutes. As the average height of a man was 5' 6" this makes the average bow about 5'10". It was termed a 'self bow', and is made from a single piece of wood, the best being Spanish yew. But by the 1500s this was a rare commodity and ash, elm or wych hazel were suitable alternatives. The stave would be at best 'three fingers thick' and clean of knots if possible. They would be cut to a 'D' cross section with the sapwood to the outer edge and the hardwood to the belly to add power. A good bow would pull up to 120lbs, any more would have been too tiring to shoot for any period of time. The string was made from hemp and protected from the elements by a 'glewe' of beeswax and tree oils. A good bowman would carry spare strings under his hat to keep them dry.

The arrows were made of aspen, poplar, birch or ash, fitted with swan, goose or peacock feathers as flights. It is no coincidence that swans and geese are a common sight on Linlithgow Loch even today. Not only were they good food for the Palace residents but they also provided a ready source of flight feathers. The distance between the stave and the string when the bow was spanned determined the length of the arrow shaft, generally around 24". They were fitted with iron 'bodkin' heads; long needle like, heads with a square cross section. This equated to the medieval version of the armoured piercing bullet.

The weapon's effective range would be some 250 to 300yds but at Flodden the effectiveness was reduced by the weather, the use of the pavises and modern armour. The favoured tactic was to shoot en masse, drawing the bow to the ear before releasing at a steady rate 10 - 12 arrows a minute. This took training and confidence under battle conditions. We can assume the small ill trained numbers at Linlithgow would not be as effective. However the combination with the other missile weapons would have been at the least disconcerting for the well-armoured man (lethal to the unarmoured levy) at maximum range and the equivalent of a deadly sniper at close range.

The Crossbow

Hand in hand with the development of the bow was that of the crossbow. The favoured European weapon due to its ease of use and simpler manufacture, the crossbow had evolved into a weapon of compatible power to the bow. Its only drawback was the poor rate of fire (4 - 6 bolts a minute depending on the strength and mechanism of the bow) and the subsequent need for protection on the battlefield. The weapon was highly suited to skirmishing, as it could be carried loaded. Once released, the crossbowman could then look for cover to reload. The Swiss again were great exponents of the crossbow but by the 1500s were replacing them with firearms.

Certainly the Borderers would have carried a crossbow or 'latch' strapped to their saddles as a one shot weapon.

Interestingly, the Accounts of the Lord High Treasurer of Scotland record that on 19th July 1526:

'To William Dully till by stringis to the kingis crossbowis and graithing[38] thame.'[39]

One can imagine that Master Dilly was first to the call when raising the Edinburgh militia and survived the action at Linlithgow as at Christmas of the same year he was paid £5 6s 6d for 'livery clothis issued William Dilly, crocebowman'. The records also record payment to Henry Wilson, a crossbowmaker, who on 19th October 1526 was paid for supplying a crossbow to the King or more likely to his guardian, Angus.

Shotte

An alternative candidate for the favoured missile weapon would have been the Harquebus or Hackbut. This was the grandfather of the musket and son of the medieval hand gun. Although the use of firearms had been around for a century it was only in the early 1500's that the gun was seen as a valid replacement for the bow and crossbow. In 1525, one year before Linlithgow, the power of this new weapon in the right hands had been clearly demonstrated at the Battle of Pavia where the might of the French cavalry had been cut down, not by the bowmen of the English, but by the light mercenary troops of the Italian Landsknechts. Undoubtedly the French advisors of the Royal court would have recounted this defeat and would have encouraged the Scots to follow suit. However our interpolation exercise would suggest otherwise. Certainly the Scottish army at Flodden looked to artillery and not the hackbut to provide their firepower and surprisingly the same can be said for Pinkie. The English were slow off the mark deploying only some 600 harquebusiers in the latter battle, but there is distinctly little reference made to the effectiveness of Scottish gunners. Contemporary illustrations clearly show English skirmishes firing into the pike but there are no signs of their counterparts in the Scottish ranks.

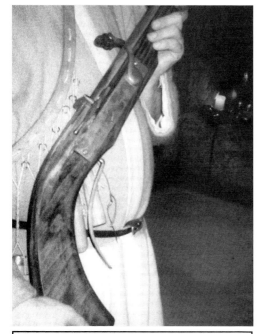

This close up of the harquebus clearly shows the firing mechanism, serpentine, pan and trigger. The use of 'apostles', measured containers of powder slung around the body, in this period is dubious. (Authors Collection)

The weapon consists of a metal barrel about a metre long mounted on a thick wooden stock and connected to a trigger and hahn or serpentine. The hahn had a hole in it through which a lighted match was secured by means of a threaded key. The match was made of a hemp rope soaked in saltpetre and be kept smouldering when lit by gently blowing on the end. A small pan was fitted to the barrel covering a hole. Gunpowder was poured into the barrel, followed by the ball enveloped in linen or wadding. The ball was rammed home using a wooden rod. Gunpowder would then be placed in the pan, covered until required and when aimed the match was then lowered into the pan by depressing the trigger which in turn rotated the cock. The powder in the pan would ignite the powder in the barrel firing the ball and wadding. The weapon would usually be fired from the waist or chest as it lacked the accuracy to warrant an aimed shot from the shoulder. The effective range was around 150yds, easily penetrating armour and could wound an unarmoured man at twice that range.

Harquebusier demonstrating his craft *'Would to God that this unhappy weapon never been devised, and that so many brave and valiant men had never died in the hands of those who were often cowards and shirkers, who would never dare to look in the face those whom they lay low with there wretched bullets. They are tools invented by the devil to make it easier for us to kill each other'*

The 'despised' gunner showing off the tools of his trade. Note the heart on the sleeve indicating he fights for the Douglases. (Tony Pollard's Collection)

If the actual firing of the weapon seemed complicated, if not requiring too much skill, the use of effective drill on the field was even more difficult to master. Volley firing or a rolling discharge of shot, took a great deal of training and required a cool head under fire. The most common tactic was that of skirmishing ahead of the main body attempting to disrupt enemy movement and weaken their resolve. The noise and smoke alone would seriously dent the moral of the less fervent participants. We can therefore believe that the small numbers of harquebusiers at Linlithgow would have been best suited to this role.

Artillery

When James IV marched south to Flodden he took with him one of the most powerful artillery trains seen in Europe. There were 5 cannon (firing 60 pound shot), 2 culverins (18lb shot) 4 culverins pickmoyen (7lb shot) and 6 culverins moyen (4lb shot). The movement of this arm itself was a tremendous logistical effort, the cannons and culverins alone requiring a team of 36 oxen, served by 9 drivers and 30 pioneers.

This is not to mention the artillery workshop, 28 pack horses to carry the shot, twelve carts of gunpowder, twenty six gunners and 300 other men.

James had embraced the modern technology of the time, employing the greatest craftsmen around, managed by Robert Borthwick his 'master meltar', to build up such an impressive armoury. The Treasury Rolls clearly detail fairly regular payments of his salary of £100 a year a tidy sum for the period and issue of livery. There are also frequent payments for materials and wages for his gunners and gunhouse as well as for the actual supply of guns. Borthwick was certainly busy in his undertakings:

'deliverit to Robin Borthwick ,master founder gunner to furnish stokkis, ire, charcole and uthir necessaries for the founding of certane gunnies in the castell [Edinburgh] be the ressate Pevis his servitour'[41]

The accounts of the Lord High Chancellor for May of 1526 details the payments to the messengers despatched to find Lord Borthwick, 'maister gunnar' and bring him back to the capital. Presumably he was set to work stocking up the arsenal as subsequent payments for 4 Falcons being built in the castle appear. The accounts also detail the money spent in providing the horses and carts to bring the wood for the gun mounts in from 'Scherefhau', the iron to make the mountings and the smithy's wages, and subsequent transport of six guns in late June to the 'East'. Along with Borthwick appear the names of Sir Alexander Jardin, John Cunningham, Thomas Crauford and John Drummond, all artillerists in the King's pay. The same guns are interestingly shown as being repaired later that year.

The forges in Edinburgh could not keep up with the demand and many weapons were imported from the continent. Their construction was an art in itself. For most of the 1400's cannon had been cast in iron or lengths of wrought iron bound by hoops. However metal fatigue would set in after a number of firings often resulting in a catastrophic explosion. It was possible to fire great weights of shot a considerable distance, quite capable of bringing down the strongest of castle defences.

Mons Meg is the best known of these weapons, weighing in at an impressive 8 1/2 tons capable of firing the 18" diameter stone ball over 2,800 yds. But its use as a field weapon was limited.[42]

By the late 15th century barrels were being cast in one piece from bronze, a more reliable alternative. Bronze could be cast more accurately, suffered less from stress and tended to give an indication of impending failure by swelling at the breech. And being stronger they could take more powder and fire iron shot rather than stone. Cannons came in all shapes and sizes as the artillery train at Flodden demonstrates. Generally the terminology depended on the shot size, from Falconet at 1lb, Falcons at 3lbs, Sakers at 6lbs, Culverins and Cannon from 15 to 25 lbs (culverins differed from a cannon in length of the barrel). Finally the double cannon fired an impressive 100lb shot.

Bronze was not cheap, monarchs often resorting to melting down the bells from their own and enemy's churches to make good the force in times of war. Cannons certainly represented status, often grandly designed in the form of mythical beasts or devils. Many others bore names such as 'The Lion' (which gained particular recognition after it exploded on firing at the siege of Roxburgh, killing James II),'Great Devil', 'Queen' and 'Bumble bee' and were written about with affection.

To receive an artillery salute was a great honour indeed and a sure fire way to impress the visitors. Interestingly there is an account of Master James Crombie, the head usher at Linlithgow Palace, being accused of treason in 1540 for:

'treasonably holding Linlithgow Palace in defiance of the King and his authority, the King being actually and personally present as displayed by his banner, for attempting to shoot the King and his company then being in Linlithgow and for all that followed this action.'

Whether this was as some suggested a salute to his majesty's arrival which went badly wrong or as a case of 'Blue on Blue' in the battle itself we are not told but Crombie, as Baillif of Linlithgow, was great friends with James Hamilton of Finnart and it was this act that led in some part to Finnart's execution for treason.

Use of guns on the battlefield was altogether another art. James's guns at Flodden had put on a good show but they were rendered useless by their positioning. Hall's account describes the artillery duel;

'out brast the ordinance on both sides with fire flame and hideous noise,'[43]

Not to mention the palls of thick black smoke and acrid smell of powder. But the heavy Scottish guns were too high up the slope and unable to depress the muzzles low enough with most of their shot flying harmlessly over the heads of the English and the heavy shot burying itself in the marshy ground rather than bouncing into the targets. Scottish gunners were used to siege warfare; slow deliberate well aimed shots where time is not an issue and not the rapid fire required on the battlefield. Their lighter English counterparts easily silenced these big guns. Borthwick lived to fight another day and would have learnt a costly lesson from Flodden.

We have scant written evidence for the use of artillery at Linlithgow. Translations of Pitscottie's accounts refer to Lennox approaching the town with his men:

'well furnist with artallaize'[44]

and later as the Douglases and the King approached the battlefield:

'They hard the artaillze schot on baitht the sydis lykeas it had been thundar'[45]

Suggesting Arran too had artillery at hand.

Leslie's account refers to Arran's force being armed with

'Speir, sword and Gunn'[46]

however this could refer simply to firearms and not artillery.

In addition, we have to consider where these pieces came from. The wonderful artillery train that James IV had at Flodden had been lost and his big pieces would have been difficult to replace. We also know that Albany took artillery on his unsuccessful expedition to Wark in

Light Artillery This replica is housed at the Flodden Museum in Etal Castle. These light mobile guns could easily be manoeuvred alongside the advancing pike blocks and provide devastating supporting fire. (Authors Collection)

The Tantallon Gun This replica of a breach loading artillery piece is in Tantallon Castle and is typical of the small guns held in the garrison's arsenal. Such guns could be easily mounted on carriages and taken on campaign (Authors Collection)

1523, so some pieces were available and most likely held at Edinburgh. But Douglas reportedly heard gunfire on his way to the battle whilst one assumes, escorting the field pieces from Edinburgh. So Arran must have procured cannon from somewhere else. The Palace would have been the ideal place. Certainly Linlithgow was a renowned Royal arsenal for many years. The Exchequer rolls of 1458 record a payment to John of Dunbar for the repairs he made to a great bombard and other instruments in the arsenal at Linlthgow.[47] But since the death of James IV, the Palace has stood empty, with little more than a caretaker staff and apart from the aforementioned incident with Master Crombie, there appears to be no account of guns being held there. An alternative source for the guns would have been Blackness Castle, renowned for its security and destined to be the great 'unsinkable' artillery fortification in James V's reign. Lighter guns from here could certainly have been moved to Linlithgow in time to join Arran's defensive line.

Lennox's procurement of guns is easier to explain. Mustering his troops at Stirling meant easy access to the arsenal there. Even so he apparently had trouble ensuring they remained there as Douglas tried to recover the pieces. Pitcairn's Criminal Trials for 1526 lists the details of the case of:

> 'Robert Bruce of Erthe and Mr Thomas Bruce and James Bruce of Mungowellis, his brothers, received the King's respite for art and part of the stouthrief (violent robbery) of certain mangonels and artillery coming from the Castle of Stirling to the King's Majesty at his burgh of Edinburgh for the defence of his person.'[48]

The same rebels were accused of robbing 'the King's letters from his officers and laying violent hand upon them' inferring the escort did not give up their property without a fight. We can only presume the crime was in some way sponsored by the rebels or at least the brigands were stealing to order.

But this was to be a rapid advance on Edinburgh; a grand show of force enough to wrest the King from the Douglases and the last thing he would have wanted was a drawn out siege. The likelihood is that Lennox would have brought the lighter guns with him, intending to make a big noisy impression and not to use as a major arm in a pitched battle.

The most compelling evidence for the presence of artillery is the discovery of a number of cannon balls by Mr David Clelland, a local historian. The smaller 11oz iron ball, the size of an

Cannon Balls found along the River Avon These two cannon balls were found along the banks of the Avon. The shot on the left is sized for a saker, the one on the right is likely to be for a quarter falcon or falconette and has been flattened on one side through impact. (Authors Collection)

orange, is flattened at one side and probably fired from a Quarter Falcon. The ball was found in the shale along the Avon between the Burgh Mills and the Nunnery. A 5lb ball, probably from a Saker, was found at the Burgh Mills. As there has been little further occasion for the discharging of cannon balls in the vicinity of the bridge, it can be safely assumed that these are from the battle.

On the basis of the foregoing it seems likely that artillery was available to both sides. t Arran's initially set up a number of heavier guns at the bridge in prepared positions with Lennox deploying similar guns as counter artillery fire on Manuel Hill. Perhaps both these and lighter guns were redeployed during the flanking attack, Lennox finding them difficult to manoeuvre in the marshy ground and Arran trying not to repeat the errors the Scots made in siting the guns at Flodden. Certainly these pieces would have added to the noise and smoke on the field

Cavalry

As much as the Scots clung on to the use of the spear over the the diversity of polearms they also consistently failed to produce a good cavalry arm. Contrary to popular belief this was not primarily due to the lack of interest by the gentry. James IV had embraced the need of a strong cavalry arm as he had the use of Pike. His accounts and letters clearly show him importing good quality horses from France and Aragon. There were Royal stud farms set up at Doune, Dundee and Newark. He used the Rapploch in Stirling to graze his stud and the ground floor of the Linlithgow Palace sported a fine set of stables where the King kept his Bey gelding, black horse and his white nag.[49]

But training horses for battle was a long and expensive business. The gentry of the land would certainly ride to the battle but without the training in the tactics of charging home knee to knee with their colleagues, they would revert to the 'traditional' method of fighting on foot. This would be particularly so if the bulk of the retinue fought dismounted and this would ensure they did not risk their expensive mounts.

There was no lack of horses in the borders either. Trade with England, be it legal or not, was thriving and the Border horseman depended on his cob, hobbie and Galloway. It was said that the local levy when called to the 'Hot Trod' could easily raise 2000 mounted men in less than 24 hours. Unfortunately they tended to disperse with the same ease once the battle had been won.

Flodden had been the last 'bow and bill' battle for the English, their men at arms preferring to join the foot soldiers and carry polearms. The only contingent of horse on the field was the 200 border horse commanded by Lord Dacre. By the time of Pinkie, the English man at arms had returned to the saddle, all be it supported by German mercenaries. Even so these numbers were woefully inadequate compared to the continental armies of the time. The Scots however had no cavalry at all at Flodden and very few in a fit state to fight at Pinkie after a brush with the English the previous night. However Pitscottie makes a surprising reference when discussing Lennox's troops mustering in Stirling;

> 'and the maister of Kilmaures mett him with tuo thousand horsemen and tuik his [Lennox's] vangaird in hand and cam forwardis.'[50]

It would have made perfectly good tactical sense for these mounted men to stay with their master[51] and act as a reconnaissance force ahead of the army's advance. It was probably they who discovered Arran's army entrenched at the bridge and the ford at Manuel. However there is little other reference so one can assume that due to the marshy conditions across the river they either dismounted to fight on foot or played no further part in the battle as a cavalry arm.

Uniforms and Clothing

By 1500 there was a new fashion house on the streets of Edinburgh. Very much like today, the big players in fashion designed for the upper echelons in France, Italy and Spain. However unlike today, the influence from Europe was stifled by the politics and communications of the period. There certainly was a sense of keeping up with the Valois's when it came to the higher classes but for many of the lower orders there were still vestiges of regional medieval costume.

As a commoner it was usual to wear a limited wardrobe, the standard linen or cotton shirt worn low on the neck and 'braes', double 'hose' (the forerunner of trousers) made of wool and possibly lined. These were strung to a waistcoat or sleeved doublet by a set of 'points' Over the doublet and most likely for early September, a tunic, jerkin or jacket would be worn. A cloak would be worn during the day and used as blanket at night. On the head was worn a coif or small cap fashionable with a turned up brim. Older men wore a soft square cap.

Livery

On reporting to the muster the levy may have been issued or asked to bring with them the only vestige of 'uniform' on show. A full-

The Drummer This statue of a drummer is taken from the fountain in Linlithgow Palace built around 1538. The fountain was the centrepiece of the restoration of the Palace during James V's reign and clearly reflects the typical military clothing of the period. (Authors Collection)

skirted tunic or frock in the colours of the household field from the coat of arms was a common form of identity. The Hamiltons dressed in red[52] with white trim, the 'Red' Douglases favouring red and white and Lennox in white with red trim. In addition a household mark or badge would have been sewn onto the clothes. Appendix 7 details the most likely badges and colours for the families involved. The Cinquefoil was the mark of the Hamiltons, Lennox had been using a red rose long before it became a mark of the Tudor dynasty and the Douglas's bearing a red heart. As both sides believed they fought for the Scottish monarchy, the national symbol of the white saltire would have been misleading.

It was also common for armies to take field signs for the day, such as a sprig of foliage worn in the hat or a strip of white cloth tied around the arm. There is no record of this being the case at Linlithgow but as both sides looked alike then such a mark would have been useful.

A more well to do gentleman may have succumbed to the latest fashion sweeping Europe. It is thought that the Swiss and German Landsknechts whilst on campaign had made captured clothes fit by slashing the garments. This craze, fuelled by the fearsome reputation these troops had across Europe, soon spread. Slashes showed not only the opulence of the attire, but that the wearer could afford the realms of material in such baggy style and could also show the rich lining as well. Whether a member of the Scottish gentry could feel 'hip' enough to go to the extravagant extremes being witnessed on the battlefields of Italy, such as wearing only one leg

James Hamilton of Finnart This superb recreation of James Hamilton of Finnart shows the detail of his attire. This nobleman supports the finest velvet surcoat and top quality armour.
(Authors Collection.)

of the hose and exposing the other or bearing the cheeks of your bottom through the seat of the garment, would have been doubtful especially considering the Scottish climate. But certainly they would have adopted baggy appearance and a modest degree of slashing.

Heads of the household would have taken these styles to their zenith by combining practicality of campaign dress with the opulence of their class. It must be remembered that such forays witnessed at Linlithgow were more a matter of political statement than of military strategy. The show of grandeur was as important as the show of arms. The Lairds would have been dressed in the finest material, surcoats of silk lined with furs and adorned with the finest embroidery in coloured silks and gold or silver thread. A style known as Blackwork, where black silk thread stitched in the pattern of scrolls adorned the finest silk shirts, was very popular. Quilting and padding enhanced the more manly features.

The rigours of a long campaign would have taken its toll on the grandeur of the clothing, but the rescue of the King was to be more of a hit and run raid, taking no more than a few weeks at the most. Certainly the use of force was the prime objective but there would be no compromise on looking the part of the King's rightful guardian

Plaids And Kilts
Much credit must be given to Hollywood in perpetuating the myth that Scots wore kilts as far back as Wallace. This is simply not true. There are descriptions of Scottish dress which may be misinterpreted as the wearing of a kilt but in the main, the nearest one can get is to the style of wearing the shirt long and dispensing with the hose and going bare legged. The earliest definitive recorded use of the belted plaid can be attributed to Gaelic sources dated 1594. We can therefore dismiss any notion that our combatants at Linlithgow wore any form of plaid or kilt.

Armour and Accoutrements
The nobleman who was off to war would have donned his most prized armour. Unlike his grandfathers though this armour would have been lighter and stronger. Often described as a 'white harness' the fully armoured man would carry a weight of 25 - 35 kgs of plate armour. New technology and improvements in production meant that the armour of the 15th century was fully articulated and covered every part of the body. Contrary to modern myth a fully armoured knight could easily get back to his feet if knocked down and demonstrate tremendous agility when in combat. Certainly by Flodden the armoured gentleman would

Fluted Armour This replica fluted German armour is on display in the Flodden Museum at Etal Castle and is typical of the period. (Authors Collection)

have worn what is known as three quarter plate either in the Milanese style or perhaps the more expensive fluted Gothic style. The standard harness would have consisted of a bevor to protect the neck, front and back plate, plackart across the stomach, fauld and tassets to cover the hips and upper legs. His arms would have supported pauldrons across the shoulders and upper and lower arm armour. Articulated metal gauntlets protected the hands. Lower legs once protected by greaves may well have been left exposed to aid fighting on foot. The fluted curved plates were designed to deflect sword blows and arrow strikes leaving the wearer relatively safe.

Suit of plate armour This replica armour on display in the Flodden Museum in Etal Castle, is typical of the half armour worn by the front ranks of Scottish troops in the pike blocks (Authors Collection)

However by the 15th Century the steady introduction of gunpowder and the growing effectiveness of the gun were starting to negate the protection afforded by plate and by 1547 at Pinkie it was noted that the common man wore similar amounts of armour to his more illustrious lord. Cost also had a part to play. The revolution in manufacturing armour abroad meant that cheap 'Almenis' armour was exported to Scotland. James IV had set up his own armour mill at Stirling and had paid French armourers to work there. This meant that a lord could stock pile large amounts of plate armour for use by his retinue.

Armour and Swords Re-enactor's collection of armour and equipment that would most likely be used in 1526. Much of the equipment dates back to the late 15th Century but the square topped 'almein' armour and the German short sword are very much in the style of 1526. (Authors Collection)

Those not fortunate enough to be handed out a harness at the muster could have brought alternatives with them. Aketons had been the favoured poor man's armour since the days of Robert The Bruce. Aketons were made of layers of canvas or linen stuffed with horse hair, hay rags or wool and usually stitched vertically to retain their shape. They smelt, got heavy when wet but made a good mattress in the evenings. They could protect the wearer from cuts and glancing blows but were useless against shot. In an attempt to stiffen the armour plates of metal were stitched into the linings of cloth armour giving it an 'upholstered' look. These coats of plates or 'jacks' were cheap and practical, comfortable to wear and surprisingly effective. They were the chosen protection for the border horsemen and many of the foot. By the time of Pinkie the majority of Scottish soldiers were wearing a jack. Arran, for example, was fitted out with a Jack with splints[53] on the arms and an apron of plate.[54] The chroniclers put the heavy number of casualties to the Scottish nobility down to the fact that they were clothed in very similar armour to the common soldier and were put to the sword rather than taken for ransom.

And of course there was the reliable chain mail. Popular since the Roman times chain mail haulberks were flexible, offered good protection against cuts and slashing but were vulnerable to puncturing by arrows and of course were useless against shot. They were also relatively expensive and heavy.

The wise soldier would wear a combination of armour, chain and padded jacks along with areas of plate. It depended very much on what he could afford or what was available from the muster. Very few would have gone completely unarmoured into combat

Finally the soldier would carry a helmet. Many contemporary woodcuts show combatants wearing civilian caps and appearing unarmoured. What is more likely is that he wears a skull cap under the bonnet. No more than a metal dome it provided adequate protection as well as facilitating the pursuit of fashion.

A more traditional style was the kettle helmet. The dome of the skull cap was supplemented with a brim. This not only protected the wearer from cuts across the face and neck but also shielded the eyes from the sun and more appropriate in Scotland stopped the rain running into the eyes. More importantly the helmet allowed good vision and hearing as well as being relatively lightweight. Any blow was deflected off the dome and rim beyond the collarbone, thus preventing a disabling injury. So popular and effective was the design that the British armed forces retained the shape right into the 1950s.

However, kettle helmets were evolving. The brims were being set at an angle and joined to the front and back of the helmet. This was the forerunner to the popular morion of the later 16th Century. Cheek guards were being added to protect against blows across the face but nasel bars although not unknown were rare. The ridge of the helmet was often strengthened by means of a raised spine or comb. The slot at the rear of the comb allowed for the addition of a plume of ostrich feathers, very nice on parade but very impractical during a campaign.

A derivation of the combed helmet was the borderers'steel bonnet' just coming into popularity. In this case the combed dome was given a peak instead of a brim and cheek guards. This style became the hallmark of the border reivers of the following years but was not common sight in 1526.

Gentlemen in full armour favoured the enclosed helmets of their forefathers. Rounded face visor, holed to allow for ventilation seemed to be the most fashionable style, although more angular helmets of the 15th Century were too valuable to leave at home for the sake of fashion. Sallets, which had been around for some 150 years were still popular. They could be left open with no face protection or fitted with fixed or moveable 'jaw bone' visors. The sallet combined with a bevor could in effect protect the whole face. Helmets were no doubt adorned with bandanas and plumes in the household colours to enhance recognition.

The Re-enactors from Gaddgedlar show off a variety of headgear for the period; The gunner on the right wears a skull cap under his bonnet, James Hamilton wears a jaw bone sallet and the retinue man a stylish fluted sallet of german origin (Tony Pollard's Collection)

At first glance helmets seem uncomfortable and bulky but professional soldiers looked upon them like modern motorcyclists regard their crash helmets. The made to measure helmet would have little need for padding but the 'munition' helmet would have been lined with cloth and a leather liner for comfort. The wearer may also have worn a padded cap or coif under the helmet for added comfort and cushioning from the force of blows.

Retinue Man This well equipped member of the Hamilton household prepares to hand out an assortment of weapons held in the armoury at the muster. The bulging frock suggests he wears a combination of padded, chain and plate armour under it. (Authors Collection)

33   The Historie and Cronicles Of Scotland - Vol 2" by Robert Lindsay of Pitscottie trans JG Mackay (Scottish Text Society 1899 - 1911)

34   'A history of Greater Britain, as well England as Scotland' by John Major (Edinburgh : T. & A. Constable, 1892.)

35   Currently used by the sailing club to haul their boats onto.

36   Pitscottie calls them 'Macleods and Macgregors and all the Islesmen of Scotland'

37   a fitsmele being 4 inches

38   Graithing - preparing or setting up

39   Extracts from Scottish Arms Makers by Charles E Whitelaw p.89

40   It was only recently that Arquebus balls were discovered at Flodden, up until then it was thought the guns landed by the French never made it to the battlefield -. Two Men in a Trench: Battlefield Archaeology - The Key to Unlocking the Past by Neill Oliver and Tony Pollard published by Michael Joseph - 2002

41   Accounts of the Lord High Treasurer of Scotland 1473 - 1566. Ed Thomas Dickson and Sir James Balfour Paul (Edinburgh 1877 - 1916)

42   'Scottish Weapons and Fortifications 1100 - 1800' by DH Caldwell (Edinburgh John Donald 1981)

43   'The Triumphant Reign of Kyng Henry VIII' by Edward Hall ed Charles Whitby and T.C. Jack (London 1904)

44   The Historie and Cronicles Of Scotland - Vol 2" by Robert Lindsay of Pitscottie trans JG Mackay (Scottish Text Society 1899 - 1911). Interestingly enough and some what disconcertingly, the Mackay translation replaces 'artallaize' with 'all necessaris'

45   The Historie and Cronicles Of Scotland - Vol 2" by Robert Lindsay of Pitscottie trans JG Mackay (Scottish Text Society 1899 - 1911)

46   The Historie Of Scotland - Vol 2" by Jhone Leslie Ed Thomas Thomson (Bannatyne Club 1830)

47   Exchequer Rolls of Scotland 1264 - 1600 Ed J Stuart et al (Edinburgh 1878 - 1908).vi 385

48   Criminal Trials In Scotland from 1488 to 1624" Ed. Robert Pitcairn, (Edinburgh 1833) Bannatyne and Maitland Clubs 1829 - 1833,

49   'Linlithgow Palace - History and Traditions' By Ferguson (Edinburgh & London, [1910])

50   The Historie and Cronicles Of Scotland - Vol 2" by Robert Lindsay of Pitscottie trans JG Mackay (Scottish Text Society 1899 - 1911)

51   Earl of Glencairn and the Laird Of Kilmauris are father and son, the title of Earl being bestowed on the family to the Laird after the Siege of Boness in 1487 by James III

52   Pitscottie describes Arran on finding Lennox's body as 'laid his cloak of skarlet vpoun him.'However this is more likely referring to the type of cloth rather than the colour.

53   Splints in this case were plates of metal attached to the arms of the jack by points and interconnected by chain.

54   TA ix 97 98 112 out of 'Scotland and War' by MacDougall (Edinburgh : John Donald, 1991) p75

Chapter 9
'So Many Brave and Valiant Men'
The Use of Mercenaries and Professional Soldiers from France

European armies of the early renaissance were multinational affairs; professional mercenaries formed the mainstay of most forces. The Swiss and Germans looked upon the course of war as a recognised form of national income. The great Italian states possessed no standing army of their own, preferring to hire men when called for. The end of the Hundred Years War saw the prevalence of fighting men who roamed Europe looking for military employment and if left unemployed for too long resorted to instigating their own form of self employment.

Ironically a year before Linlithgow the Duke of Albany was pitched into the forefront of mercenary combat in the campaign in Italy fighting for the French King. He was tasked to take a force of some 600 Frenchmen, 4,000 Lankschnechts, 300 light cavalry and 100 men at arms to the relief of Naples. March and countermarch ensured a strategic victory for the Scot but it also shows how a commander of the period would be expected to lead such an assorted company of nationalities.

The French army of 1523

Despite the resounding demand for French arms and equipment from the Scottish nobles the average French army left a lot to be desired. The French contingent sent to Scotland in 1523 was a mix and match of mercenaries and French officers. It was estimated to be some 4,000 strong, predominantly infantry but with 100 men at arms with their attendants. Eighty barded horses provided the mounted arm. Artillery consisted of 20 large cannons and four double cannons. Inventory also included many 'pavaises' and most unusually a 'fort of artillery' most likely a war wagon. It was also noted that there was a plentiful supply of powder and guns and twelve vessels carried wine and victuals. Margaret in a letter to Surrey also refers to 3,000 Germans or Swiss on the way who, had they arrived, would have made a very potent force indeed.

The most potent arm was the cavalry, consisting of the 'lances' of noble men and their 'archers' in this case not bowman, but valets or couteilleurs. There was no native light cavalry arm. The French preferred to hire Venetian 'stradiots' or depended on mounted crossbowman. As the 16th Century wore on the crossbow was replaced by pistoleers or arquebus, almost as difficult to use on horseback as their predecessor.

The infantry arm was of poorer quality. The pike was initially hired in from Switzerland with the only Frenchmen being the Gascon crossbowmen escorting them. Arquesbusiers were a rare breed in the early 16th Century. Montluc remarks in his memoirs in 1523 that his company of over 100 only had 6 gunners all of whom were Spanish. Montluc adds;

' Would to God that this unhappy weapon never been devised, and that so many brave and valiant men had never died in the hands of those who were often cowards and shirkers, who would never dare to look in the face those whom they lay low with their wretched bullets. They are tools invented by the Devil to make it easier for us to kill each other'. [55]

Gunners were still hated and despised and the French were still slow to pick up on the awesome effect of mass ranks of guns until Pavia in 1525 when their allied mercenaries and noble gendarmes were mown down by men no more than brigands.

Gunners needed the protection of their pikes when threatened by cavalry on a regular basis. However the French pikeman was regarded as a poor substitute for the mercenary, often the new recruit preferring to take up the gun. The average pikeman was hired more for his brawn than his soldiering ability. They also suffered from lack of experience being raised in times of trouble and disbanded once peace returned. The first real attempt of organising a standing French army was in 1531 when Francis I created 'Legions' in the manner of the Romans of up to 6,000 strong.

The apparent poor reputation of the French infantry did not prevent James IV employing 40 French military advisors under D'Aussi to train his pike blocks, each block being controlled by eight of these men at Flodden. It was these men who took the blame for the defeat of the pike blocks, some being murdered on the field of battle for the results of their coaching.

When it came to artillery though, French experience and skills were second to none. The campaigns in the Italian wars had given the French artillerists the perfect opportunity to hone their skills. They excelled at the battles of Ravenna in 1512 and perhaps more pertinently to Linlithgow, Marignano in 1525 where the French gunners loaded and manoeuvred quicker than any before then. James IV had steadily been building up the arsenal under the guidance of French gunners. There are a stream of French and Dutch gunners mentioned in government records leading up to Flodden. Men like John Veilneif who was in charge of casting at Stirling, and a certain Gerwez who transferred the gunmaking workshops to Edinburgh by 1511. Then there was George Keppin and his servant Kasper Lepus who maintained the Edinburgh arsenal up to 1515.

It is safe to assume that the defeat of Wark and public embarkation of the French contingent from Leith did not see the end of the French presence within the Scottish ranks. Households would employ continental officers and men to supplement their depleted retinues. Gunners would be instructed by French officers, sergeants and 'whifflers' would bark out orders in all the languages of Europe. The ranks at Linlithgow would have a fair smattering of foreign officers and men to add a degree of professionalism.

55 'Commentaires by Monluc, Blaise de Lasseran-Massencôme, seigneur de

Chapter 10
'Come to Edinburgh witht all the powar that he might be'
Logistics of the Campaign

Every army needs its supplies and typically the baggage following the Renaissance army would be enormous. But things were different for the combatants at Linlithgow. Both armies would have mustered with a set period of campaign in mind, the troops were asked to bring enough supplies for the immediate days campaigning. Lennox as the antagonist and premeditator, planned for a quick and perhaps bloodless march on Edinburgh taking no more than a week or fighting his decisive battle before then. He had many supporters en route and expected these households to provide supplies. Allies such as the Laird of Houston had estates on the march that could have provided refuge and supplies for the rebels. Some burghs and households arranged supplies in lieu of manpower or contributed financially to pay for the provisions.

Known Douglas sympathisers provided another source of plunder. However Lennox was wary to let his men off the leash as he had one eye on the future and tried to raise as much support for his cause on the march as he could. Pillaging only alienated any potential allies. It was a burden enough to have an army of 10,000 billeted in the burgh.

It is therefore easy to imagine Lennox's troops carrying everything they needed with them. Fodder for the horses, personal supplies of beer, wheat, bread, cheeses and salted meat all strapped to the saddles or carried on the back. As the march got underway it would be feasible for the household retainers to be re-supplied directly from their estates by runner. The only carts required would be for the artillery ammunition, the pikes and perhaps tentage. Scottish soldiers were adept at creating crude shelters out of wood and turf when the army stopped for the night

Douglas on the other hand was fighting with diminishing supply lines and with plenty of Royal estates to bed down in. Linlithgow at the time was not being used as a residence but the payment rolls suggest it was being stocked with provisions. And we know after the battle the King and Douglas retired to the palace to hold a celebrative party again suggesting there was plenty to feast on. Likewise Linlithgow was a Hamilton town with many of the houses owned by kinfolk. There would be plenty of billets for the mustering troops here.

It must also be remembered that Arran's troops who did the bulk of the fighting for the Douglas's were all locally raised and may have slept in their own houses the night before. Both sides would march fresh and fight with full bellies.

Chapter 11
'Come and Burieit Him'
The Dead and Dying

We know little of the actual numbers of casualties but Pitscottie and Leslie refer to many casualties among the gentlemen on both sides. This was to be expected as they stood in the front lines of the battle and been more committed to the cause than perhaps the retinue troops and levy to the rear.

By the early evening the battlefield was strewn with equipment, weapons, especially pikes, with the dead and dying and the living picking through the corpses. The final resting place would depend very much on an individual's social standing and whose side they were on.

For the nobleman on the winning side the family and retinue had time to recover the body, protect the personal possessions and arrange for the return to the family home. Lesser men were laid out for recognition and as many of the combatants came from local households it is most likely that the family were on hand to claim the body. The foreign and professional troops were looked after by their colleagues, arrangements made for a decent burial and the possessions split among their comrades.

Linlithgow may well be noted for its treatment of the losing nobleman. This was very much a personal affair, the leading players on both sides were fighting men they knew as allies just months before. We know that Lennox's body was visited by Arran who laid his coat over the corpse. Pitscottie's description does open up the possibility of Lennox being buried on site. He describes Arran as ordering guards to watch the body until:

'the kingis servandis come and burieit him'

As this original site is now under a housing estate it would be interesting to contemplate that this man's final resting place is appropriately under a rose bed in a back garden. Photographs taken prior to the building of the estate in 1977 show quite a substantial mound, reputedly Lennox's cairn, which may have included more bodies than just Lennox.

The lesser men would not have been so fortunate. Stripped of valuables and clothes they would more likely end up in a mass grave nearby. Locals in Linlithgow suggest one such grave pit was in the Justin Haugh (or Jousting Haugh) Drive as bones were found during the building of the houses in 1938. There is no substantiated evidence to this though. The most likely place for a pit would be on the consecrated ground of the Manuel convent, however as most of the cemetery was washed away in the floods it is unlikely there are traces to be found today.

The fate of the wounded was also dependant on class. For many years the noble classes went to war with their highly paid 'syrgeons' and many of the accompanying clerics would have had a rudimentary understanding of medical practices. King James's personal physician, one Doctor Arbuthnet, probably rode with the Royal party. The wives of the nobles would often train squires and pages in basic first aid as ways of improving the chance of their husbands return. Religious orders such as the Knights of St John were practiced in the treatment of the sick and wounded. A sect of the order was based in Torphichen and was on hand to aid the more fortunate as they fled the field. For the majority however it would be your colleagues who were left to clean and dress the wound as best they could before getting the casualty home or to a place of safety. Often the local religious houses became places of caring, in this case the nunnery, the Cistercian friary on the south side of Linlithgow and St Michaels. Many of the wounded were billeted in the houses of friends and supporters in Linlithgow. On the whole however there was no systematic approach to the treatment of the wounded. Many were looted, stripped of clothing and left for dead. The mild September nights did little to stop the loss of blood, The dying went on well into the night.

Combat wounds were primarily caused by bladed weapons; trauma from smashing, puncture wounds from pike, spear and arrow and incisor wounds from slashing. The injury was complicated by the presence of external clotting or internal haemorrhaging. Treatment would be limited to an examination, cleaning with water, bandaging and rest. Often the deepest cuts were clean and would knit together well if given chance to heal. Amputation would be rare unless the cut was sufficient to warrant completing the job. The open wound would then be sealed either by cauterising with a red hot iron or a covering in boiling oil.[56] This treatment often led to more agony from scalding and burns around an already inflamed area as well as leading to the wound going septic if not regularly drained of puss and cleaned.

Perhaps the most horrific death would befall those in the front ranks of the pike block, where hemmed in by colleagues to either side and behind, you would be slowly pushed onto the heads of the pikes in front of you. Once skewered on a shaft you would be helpless to avoid the second rank of pike. Casualties in such engagements were found to have up to twenty such wounds.

The casualties of this battle suffered from wounds of a relatively new nature. Artillery and harquebus shot had brought a new more complicated injury to the surgeon's table. In 1526, low velocity, large calibre wounds combined with the presence of burning and the contamination of dirty clothing or shattered armour was a new phenomenon not yet fully understood. Many physicians of the day thought that black powder was poisonous and would resort to cauterising the wound after extracting the ball with a stout 'probe' or pincers. The physicians of the Vatican recommended amputation every time to prevent the poison spreading again followed by the appliance of a red hot iron.

Once under care, the casualty was likely to be treated by the application of balms or herbal remedies as well as blood letting with leeches and the insertion of maggots to clean away the rotting flesh. Then there was always the added comfort of spells and charms. It was not surprising therefore that many trusted their luck to a wash and bandage and putting their fate in the hands of God.

Combat wounds were not limited to the effect of a weapon. Heatstroke, heart attack, crushing and suffocation were all real threats in the heaviest of the fighting. It was not unknown for bodies to be found without a wound on them, the poor unfortunate having found the pace of the battle too much and succumbing to heart failure.

All this must be seen in the light of the day-to-day threats to health. Campaign life was a breeding ground for disease. Dysentery, scurvy and typhus were all common amongst the armies of the time. However we can dismiss this in the case of Linlithgow as the campaign was over very quickly.[57]

The fate of the wounded on recovery was also potentially fraught. Naturally the professional soldiers of Germany and Switzerland were the first to insist that their sponsors provided care for the wounded and funds to see them home. The mercenaries were among the first troops to start contributing to funds to be used to care for the wounded. It was considered an insurance policy. However for many the suffering would go on long after the wound had healed. A disability without a wealthy benefactor was likely to lead to a lifetime of poverty.

56 It was not until 1536 when a French surgeon called Pare discovered after running out of oil that a balm of yolks of egg, oil of roses and turpentine did a far better job.

57 As if that was not enough the 16th Century saw the first major outbreaks of small pox, yellow fever, whooping cough, influenza and measles

Chapter 12
'Befor any Man'
Motivation and Elan

It is important to remember that the memory of Flodden was fresh on many minds, as was the defeat at Wark only the previous year. This time the enemy was to be your neighbour, your fellow veteran and in many cases, the in-laws. And for the Douglases and Hamiltons, the man you fought against on the streets of Edinburgh some mere six years earlier was now the man who was to fight alongside you.

Theoretically any man between 16 and 60 would be eligible to answer the national muster. In practice those from the lower classes were not worth consideration and were never a major component of the force. The majority of rankers came from those with land and position to be noted in the rolls of the burgh, town or church. But being on the lists did not prevent the recruit enlisting the services of a substitute through bribery or corruption. In such cases motivation to stay in the ranks beyond enrolment would be minimal.

But money isn't everything. Many were tied to their laird through tenancy agreements, family connections or legal requirement. Douglas in particular busied himself in the summer of 1526 agreeing Bonds of Amenity with the likes of Earl Of Rothes, Hamilton of Macknariston and Lord Home binding them to:

' warn him as quickly as possible of any danger or hurt to his persons land or goods which the granter might become aware and prevent such at his power and further to concur with him in defence of the King and his authority.'

This not only ensured the laird's commitment but also his many retainers beneath him.

And as previously mentioned a similar bond was signed between Lennox and the King in June 1526, that stated:

'that wc sal wys mast spccialy and above all uderis the counsell of the sayd Jhone Erll of Lennox onto the tym of owr last reucation and perfyt age, and that we sall do nothing without the awys of the sayd erll, and first and befor any man'

Interestingly it was witnessed by:

' Wylliam Master of Glencarne, Ninian Crechtoun of Bellybocht and Patrik Houston of that ilk'

All to be found subsequently in the ranks of the Lennox army.

Chapter 13
'The Maist Necessyr Brig'
The Geography of the Battlefield

Linlithgow itself lies on the main road from Stirling to Edinburgh. The valley it straddles runs East to West, bound to the north by a ridge of hills known as the Binns and the Riccarton Hills rising to some 254 metres above sea level to the south with the westerly end giving way to the Avon valley at the impressive escarpment of Cockleroy (278m). The fact that the Union Canal, the Edinburgh to Glasgow mainline and the M9 all run within a mile of Linlithgow High Street is a testament to the importance of the valley and the strategic significance of the Palace. The Loch, somewhat shallower now than in the past, not only provided good fishing for the townspeople but was a natural choke point to progress along the valley. Running west through the outer suburbs of the West Port the road of 1526 entered countryside for a mile, passed Stockbridge, before entering the cluster of houses and the Burgh mills on the east end of the bridge spanning the River Avon.

Nothing remains of the Linlithgow Bridge of 1526,[58] but according to the oldest maps, the bridge was on the site of the modern main road to Polmont. The maps also clearly show that an old cart road ran up past what is now Easter Manuel farm and hamlet of Whitecross, before passing under the watch of Haining Castle,[59] the home of the Crawfords. The bridge was a major construction for that period and something to be defended, not dismantled.

The River Avon rises from the Fannyside Loch in North Lanarkshire near Cumbernauld, runs through Slammanan and then through the impressive and very steep sided gorge at Avonbridge amd Muiravonside. It then runs swiftly towards Linlithgow Bridge under the Victorian Union Canal aqueduct and the Glasgow to Edinburgh rail viaduct. Downstream of Linlithgow the river runs wide and fast on to the Firth of Forth at Grangemouth.

James VI described the bridge at Linlithgow as:

'the maist necessyr brig standing upone ony watter within the realme'[60]

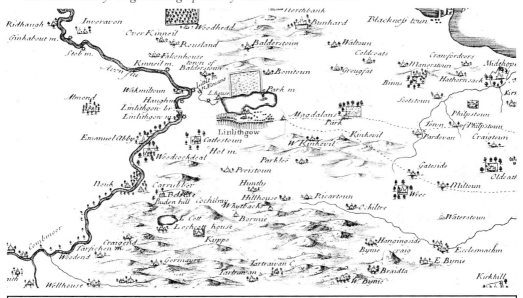

Adairs map of Linlithgow. This map clearly shows that even in 1684 there were few if any buildings between the West Port and the bridge. The only buildings of note at the river were the mills. However Kettlestoun, Woodcockdale and the Nunnery are all established landmarks. Adair has given Haining Castle its alternative name of Almond. (Reproduced by permission of the Trustees of the National Library of Scotland)

The Burgh Mills The Burgh Mills, now overshadowed by the viaduct, were the only buildings in the vicinity of the bridge that can be clearly identified as being present at the time of the action. (Authors Collection)

Avon Viaduct The viaduct bisects the battlefield. The flood plain in the middle distance is the spot now represented on the OS map by the battlefield symbol. In fact early OS maps spread the battle site along the river and beyond the main road to the north suggesting action took place either side of the bridge. (Author's Collection)

which is a good summation of the tactical importance of the position Arran took up. The water downstream is fast flowing and fordable by horse in places but certainly too risky for foot and artillery. Upstream the Avon seems peaceful but it must be recognised that in flood the river becomes a major barrier[61] and that the surrounding low lying ground is still, today, marshy and prone to flooding. Farmers now ploughing the land describe a top soil of some 12" deep before you hit the boulders and rocks, evidence of the meandering path of the river over the years.

Approximately 1.25km upstream of the bridge past the Manuel Haugh Farm stands the ruins of the Manuel Nunnery. Only the north portion of the west gable remains today but the mill and associated farm are incorporated into the small cluster of buildings to the south. The Manuel house of Cistercian nuns was founded by Malcolm IV in 1164 and confirmed by William the Lion a few years later. Little is known about the order except that the house was not wealthy and the community was always a small one. The Nunnery was mentioned in the Rag roles of Edward III who recompensed the nuns for damage his army caused on its march to Perth in 1335 but more importantly James IV raised a petition in 1506 to have the convent closed as there were little more than five nuns and they appeared to lead a life remote from the Cistercian teachings. It was granted but appears never to have been enforced as records show that the prioress and four nuns were in residence in 1552, obviously none the worst for their involvement in the battle.

Manuel Convent The ruins of Manuel Nunnery in the 18th Century before the flood in 1783 washed away the south wall and cemetery leaving only the gable end we see today. (Cardonell)

The appearance of the nunnery itself is hard to imagine from the ruins today particularly as much of the eastern end and the cemetery lie under the current path of the river.[62] The riverbed is festooned with carved stonework, a testament to the power of the flood and the westerly banks rise some 6 to 10 ft above the water level. The Manuel Burn joins the River Avon approximately 70 metres upstream of the convent and although it would pose little obstacle to troops it would provide a natural reference point at which the flank march could stop. The easterly bank is bordered by fields which were once water meadows. About 100 metres north on the lightly wooded bank lies the small holding of Drum, now a home but probably a populated steading in 1526. Nearer the river lie the remains of Kettlestoun Mill and a mill run which fed the mill, again both in use at the time of the action.

Walking north along the easterly bank on what is now a public footpath it is possible to observe the most prominent feature of the landscape. The low-lying land to the east, now a flooded quarry, is enclosed by a bluff rising some 20 metres in less than 50 metres. The escarpment may have been made more severe by the quarry workings but the crucible effect is still very noticeable. Any force manning the ridge would have a clear view of Lennox's men forming up and would easily be able to bring effective fire to bear. In addition the ridge has a false crest, now extenuated by quarrying and as you reach the ridgeline the ground flattens for approximately 100 metres before climbing again onto another crest along which the Torphichen road passes. This would allow any reinforcements to form up on flat ground and still hold a defensive position.

The line of the bluff meets the Avon at what is known as Peace Hill[63] just before the bridge. This means the low-lying marshy ground is funnelled from a width of 300 metres opposite the convent into a 100 metre frontage at the foot of Peace Hill. Even today the ground is very marshy. It is this phenomenon that may have been the main reason why Arran's force was able to hold off a force three times its number.

The Torphichen road running NE to SW and the Falkirk Road, running E toW, which passes over the bridge, form two sides of an isosceles triangle with the apex meeting at the West Port

Lennox's Cairn This modern construction is approximately 100 yds from the original location and is the most tangible memorial of the battle. (Authors Collection)

The River Avon The view from the modern bridge across the Avon taken in September and showing extent of the obstacle the river posed at this time of year. (Authors Collection)

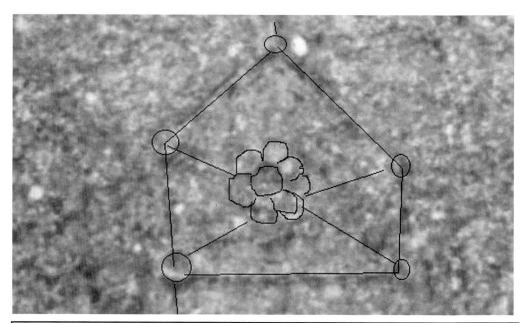

The Marker stone on the Cairn The marker stone in the Lennox Cairn. The markings, even in 1977 when it was discovered, are unclear however the general consensus was at the time that it bore the Lennox crest. (Authors Collection)

of Linlithgow Bridge. They allow quick and easy passage to both flanks of the battlefield as you pass out of the town. Standing on the Main Street in Linlithgow bridge itself is Borestane House, reputedly the location where Douglas raised his standard during the battle.

The B8528 runs NW to SE along the short third base of the 'triangle' with one point at the bridge and the other now a roundabout at the entrance to the Kettlestoun Estate and in 1526, the location of Kettlestoun Farm. This is the reputedly near the spot where Lennox was killed and is the location of Lennox Cairn a small memorial with a weather worn plaque mounted into it.[64] Many of the local road names commemorate the fight, including Lennox Gardens, Douglas Avenue, Stewart Place.

58 The modern bridge lies on the foundations of the bridge built in 1660 by the Earls Of Linlithgow

59 Haining Castle lies directly on the line of march, approximately a mile from the bridge. It was originally a 15th century manor with an L shaped ground floor and three storeys. The lands were granted to Reginald De Crauford in 1424 by the James I and remained with the Crawfords until they passed by marriage to the Lords of Callender, the Livingstones. It is also known on some maps as Almond Castle

60 'Linlithgow Palace - History and Traditions' By Ferguson (Edinburgh & London, [1910])P.144

61 As testament to the rivers potential hazard it must be remembered that both Manuel Convent and Kettlestoun Mill on the opposite bank were washed away in floods in 1783

62 Cardonnel's 'Picturesque Antiquities of Scotland' does illustrate the ruins prior to their demise in the flood . 'Picturesque antiquities of Scotland' by Adam De Cardonnel (London: : Printed for the author, and sold by Edwards, in Pall-Mall; also at Edwards's, in Halifax., M,DCC,LXXXVIII. [1788])

63 Waldie suggests Peace Hill or Peace Knowe is a derivation of the Gallic 'Bas' meaning 'death' but follows that up by saying this name probably predates the battle. The older name Pace Hill appears on many of the early OS maps. The word 'Pace' can be translated as a defile, a critical position or situation, a weight or known measure. Alternatively Pace refers to the position where the battle was concluded, or peace made. Or perhaps in a military context the place where artillery pieces were placed. It is interesting to note that Flodden too has a Pace Hill in the proximity of the fighting. It is also ironic that this is the place where Lennox's father died fighting with the Highlanders. 'History of the Town and Parish of Linlithgow' by G Waldie 3rd Edition Published 1879

64 The plaque (now embedded in the cairn) was saved from the developers' bulldozers by local historians when the farm, some 200 yds up the track, was pulled down to make way for the estate. A full and remarkable account of the history of the cairn is at Appendix 1

Chapter 14
'They Knew the Enemy Must Pass'
Dispositions and Manoeuvres

Pitscottie tells us that:

The Earle of Lennox come out of Stirling with thre great ostis...[65]

Drummond rewords Pitscottie and states that Lennox left Stirling:

'With three strong briggades he [Lennox] marched towards Linlithgow'[66]

This suggests Lennox marched in the traditional formation, splitting his force into three divisions or 'battles', that is to say; Rear, Main and Vanguard. From the same sources we are told that his force numbered some 12,000 men. It is usual for the victors to play up the numbers of the defeated force to glorify the achievement but an army of 9,000 to 12,000 men would indeed be a reasonable assumption.[67] This would mean each division if equally divided would have about 3,000 to 4,000 men. Drummond breaks it down in more detail:

'One thousand men came from the High Lands to him [Lennox], Earl of Cassilis and Master of Kilmaurus [Glencairn] com from the west with two thousand, the Queen and Archbishop James Beaton, direct from many of their vassals from Fyffe to him [Lennox].'[68]

Drummond goes on to uniquely describe the make up of each division as it marched to Manuel Convent suggesting:

'The Master of Kilmaurus [Glencairn?] gindeth the vanguard, consisting of the Westland men; the Earl of Cassilis and himself [Lennox] the main battell, many of which were highland men being of all some (as some write) 10,000.'[69]

There is no mention of the third battle previously allocated by Pitscottie to the 'Maister of Kilmaurus' with his horsemen. This suggests that this force had both been split up and absorbed into the other units, already dispersed after combat or perhaps unable to come into combat. Tytler's account may account for its demise as he suggests that the crossing of the ford at Manuel was severely contested:

'Lennox found himself compelled to attempt a passage at a difficult ford opposite the nunnery of Manuel, an enterprise by which his soldiers were thrown into disorder and exposed to severe fire from the enemy. Yet they made good their passage and some squadrons, as they pressed up the opposite bank attacked the army of Arran with great gallantry.'

The use of the word 'squadrons' here may allude to horsemen but as this account is a summation of the whole battle then it is unlikely to be that straight forward. However the forward battle could have been dispersed in the crossing and ended up joining the other two or chasing the enemy skirmishers off the heights.

Fraser's account of the fight in The Douglas Book recounts 'galling' fire as the Lennox men moved along the road to the ford again adding to the extent of the fight for the ford. Certainly the road approaching the nunnery would be in range of guns based on the heights opposite and the terrain around the river offered good cover for skirmishers to ply their trade.

Once across the ford Lennox faced another problem in deploying his remaining troops in the available space. The tactics of the day preached by the European masters were very much dictated by science and the perfection of a square pike block was tantamount. The overriding rule was the 3:7 ratio; that is to say that one man needed 3 paces width to effectively wield his weapon but in order to march without bumping into those in front and behind he needed 7 paces. By simple maths it is easy to see that a body of 21 men would form a perfect square when arrayed in 7 files and three ranks. Multiply this up then 3000 men would form a block of 84 files by 36 ranks.[70]

Assuming a pace[71] is approximately equal to a 0.91m this meant the body of men covered an area of 229 by 229 metres. Divisions formed up far enough apart to provide mutual fire support but not to get entangled on the move. We can therefore reckon the battles would have 50 metres between them. For three battles the frontage would be in the order of 787 metres. The distance between the river and the line of bluffs opposite the Nunnery is roughly 350 metres.

On crossing the ford Lennox looked to array his men facing northeast to march on Arran's position at the bridge or towards town. He found to his dismay that he could only deploy his forward and half his main battle into line abreast before the slopes stopped him. Even more worrying as he advanced north, the funnel effect of the land forced these two battles onto one another causing one to drop behind the other. In marshy ground with poorly trained troops and under fire the task was catastrophic. Alternatively the most easterly battle was forced to climb up the ridge onto the next plateau, losing sight of their colleagues and all cohesion as an effective pike block. The third battle, if it still existed as a fighting unit, would have to deploy behind the first two and therefore been as good as useless, not being able to push through the retreating masses to come into action and preventing the withdrawal of the men in front. At the point of action Lennox's superior numbers were reduced to a third, which evened the sides considerably and Arran and Angus still had the advantage of the slope of Peace Hill.

It is safe to say that Lennox was walking into a well-prepared trap. Certainly Arran, with the local Hamilton allies, was well aware of the terrain to the south of the bridge and pre-empted a flanking movement. As he watched Lennox's troops file south to Manuel Nunnery his own skirmishers and light horse used the crest of the bluff to snipe at the column and view their progress. Arran re-deployed his men, but sensibly, in the limited time he had and in order to keep the distance of march to a minimum he realigned his troops along the crest of Peace Hill facing south. This meant that the battle would have been fought on a north / south alignment. Angus's reinforcements arriving sometime that morning formed up on the left flank of Arran's men, facing south west and launching their attack on the flank of Lennox's hemmed in troops.[72]

Pitscottie is very clear about which battles fought each other:

'Be this ane post cam and schew the king that both the armies war joined, and fightand furiouslie, with the other on the wast side of Linlithgow, tuo mylles from the toun, and that the earle of Angus and the earle of Glencarne was zokit togidder, and the lord Hamiltounes force and the Earle of lennox in lyke manner and baitht fightand furieouslie.'[73]

Again the third battle is not mentioned as playing a role. That leaves Lennox's main battle clear passage to engage Arran and Glencairn's falling in on Lennox's right to face off against Angus.

An Alternative Disposition

There is however another possible scenario. Waldie's interpretation of the battle published in 1929 suggests that the orientation of the battle was different. He suggests Lennox crossed the river and forced the heights between Manuel Convent and the bridge launching an assault eastward. Ferguson in his 'Linlithgow Palace - History and Traditions' reaffirms this by suggesting Arran had:

'posted his soldiers on the circumjacent hills' and ' On the extensive haugh or plain opposite the nunnery a sharp contested battle was fought'.[74]

Both these accounts bear great resemblance to Tytler's account of the fight for the crossing.

If this was the case any Douglas reinforcements would have deployed in support of Arran's line facing Lennox's attack front on. This would have been a less devastating arrival than a flank attack but enough to tip the balance. However it does not account for Lennox's failure to dislodge a force a third of the size of his own from a position on the ridge a kilometre long. Lennox would have had the space to deploy all his divisions all be it under fire and probably found his troops overlapping the unprotected flanks of the opposition. Arran's small force would have not only vacated the higher ground on Peace Hill but would find themselves thinly spread along the ridge with their flanks unprotected.

Buchanan's account suggests a tantalising middle ground to the dispositions. He suggests:

'They [Hamiltonians] placed a small guard at the bridge and the rest of their forces on the brow of the hills, which they knew the enemy must pass'[75]

This suggests the Hamiltons took up positions along the bluffs from the bridge as far as the Torphichen road into the West Port as these were the only ways into the High Street. Buchanan goes on to suggest that once across the river:

'the Lennox men marched rapidly through a rugged road'[76][77]

At first glance the nearest thing to a 'road' would have been the A706 to Torphichen suggesting Lennox's line of attack was along this into the West Port. This would also suggest that he surmounted the ridge before heading North East. However the next line confuses matters again

'annoyed by stones thrown from the heights'[78]

The Torphichen road is not overlooked by heights at any point from Woodlescote farm opposite the nunnery to West Port. There are still traces though of a cart road running along the line of the bluffs and about halfway up them. It could be remnants of a track serving the quarry or the farm but it would fit the description perfectly. It comes out on the flat plateau in front of Peace Hill and would mean Lennox still had to fight up the remaining slope.

Buchanan's disposition can be seen as a viable compromise between the North South and East West theories and puts Lennox in the location of his memorial cairn, but still leaves Arran with the advantage of the hill. Angus is said to arrive as Lennox's men engage Arran's by

'rushing along the road'[79]

the same road along which Lennox's men advanced. This is presumably again the road out from the West Port towards Torphichen.

65 *The Historie and Cronicles Of Scotland - Vol 2" by Robert Lindsay of Pitscottie trans JG Mackay (Scottish Text Society 1899 - 1911)*

66 *'History of Scotland from the year 1423 until the year 1542' by William Drummond of Hawthornden (London Edn 1681)*

67 *An account of the battle by Albany written in the autumn of 1526 to Du Prat, Chancellor of Francis I confirms Angus's force as six or seven thousand men but states Lennox had only 4000 men. It must be remembered though that Albany's aim is to cast Angus as the leader of the 'murderous and wicked crew' now holding the King and sworn ally of Henry VIII, in order to obtain French arms and men. Stating Lennox had the 2 or 3 to 1 advantage may have given the impression that Angus was a reputable general if nothing else. - Teulet I 69: H iv 2539 Papiers d'etat…relatifs a l'histoire de l'Ecosse au XVI siecle Ed. A Teulet (Bannantyne Club, 1852 - 1860) Full transcript is at Appendix 6*

68 *'History of Scotland from the year 1423 until the year 1542' by William Drummond of Hawthornden (London Edn 1681)*

69 *'History of Scotland from the year 1423 until the year 1542' by William Drummond of Hawthornden (London Edn 1681)*

70 *'The Renaissance at War' by Thomas Arnold (Cassell & Co 2001)*

71 *Interpolated from the 'Instructions For Artillery' by Eugenio Gentilini by Thomas Arnold - The Renaissance at War' by Thomas Arnold (Cassell & Co 2001)*

72 *Certainly the surveyors of the Ordnance Survey map would agree, as they place their battlefield marker at the foot of Peace Hill.*

73 *The Historie and Cronicles Of Scotland - Vol 2" by Robert Lindsay of Pitscottie trans JG Mackay (Scottish Text Society 1899 - 1911)*

74 *'Linlithgow Palace - History and Traditions' By Ferguson (Edinburgh & London, [1910])*

75 *"The History of Scotland" - George Buchanan trans J Aikman (Glasgow and Edinburgh 1827 - 29) vol ii*

76 *Using translations of Buchanan's latin scripts can be fraught with inaccuracy as the Aikman's 1827 and the 1821 version by an unknown translator demonstrates. Aikman describes the rugged road the 1821 translation simply states 'The Lennoxians made towards their enemies' and does not mention the road.*

77 *"The History of Scotland" - George Buchanan trans J Aikman (Glasgow and Edinburgh 1827 - 29) vol ii*

78 *"The History of Scotland" - George Buchanan trans J Aikman (Glasgow and Edinburgh 1827 - 29) vol ii*

79 *"The History of Scotland" - George Buchanan trans J Aikman (Glasgow and Edinburgh 1827 - 29) vol ii*

Chapter 15
'Porpossit to Fight,'
The Timing of the Battle

There remains some confusion in the histories as to the timing of the reinforcements arriving on the battlefield. According to Pitscottie, Arran was on the field with the local Hamiltons on 3rd September. Time enough, he tells us, to send messages to Lennox asking him to think again and prepare a strong enough position to dissuade Lennox from launching a frontal assault across the bridge on his arrival. Pitscottie goes onto add that Angus

> *'past fordwart {from Edinburgh} himself witht the Homes and Karis {Kerrs}quhilk was in number 2000 men'[80]*

and that Angus is in position to do battle alongside Arran when Lennox launches his assault. Drummond's account of the action on the other hand suggests that Douglas arrived once the battle was joined and indeed that Arran was spurred on by James Hamilton of Finnart to begin the fight without waiting for Angus. It was, according to Drummond, his arrival on the battlefield to cries of 'A Douglas':

> *'at which alarum many of the High land men and Westland men turned their backs'[81]*

and prompted the disintegration of the Lennox forces.

Most historians agree that George Douglas and the King with the force from Leith and Edinburgh of around 3000 men arrived too late as the battle was over.
Pitscottie writes:

> *' Then the King raid fast to sie the manner, bot ane nother post met the king incontinent, showing him that the earle of Lennox men war fled from him, and believe he had tint the field;'[82]*

Pitscottie notes earlier that Lennox left Stirling 'on the morne'[83] (but does not state what day) and concludes with a graphic account of the party held in the evening at Linlithgow Palace by Angus and his allies. He therefore suggests a time frame in which the battle was fought.

However it is difficult to estimate when Lennox arrived at Linlithgow on the 4th September. Stirling lies approximately 21 miles from Linlithgow. Assuming Lennox planned to get a full day's march in on the 4th he would have left Stirling as soon as daylight and mustering permitted; in September that would be around 6.00 am.

There is some debate as to how far a Renaissance army could march in a day. It would all depend on the make up of the force, the ground over which they marched and the pressure they were under to keep up a good pace. For example, The Treasurer's Accounts give us an insight into a comparative march in 1496 when James IV moved his army to the siege of Heaton Castle. The forces were gathered at Restalrig just outside Edinburgh on 13 September and ended in Langton near Duns some 4 days later after covering some 56 miles, an average of 14 miles a day. This was with siege guns and all the paraphernalia of war. A similar account in 1565 of the itinerary of the Royalist army pursuing Lord Moray suggests 80 miles in 4 days. This army was not slowed by artillery and was probably mostly mounted. Likewise the English advance to Pinkie was at about 9 miles a day from the border stopping only to size up the resistance in various Scottish strongholds en route.

Could Lennox, cover some 21 miles in a single day and still fight a battle? We can only conclude that the force was well on the way before dawn, unburdened by baggage and heavy artillery and spurred on by Lennox looking to engage Arran before Angus could come to his aid. Lennox's men would have made Linlithgow late in the day and in poor condition to fight an engagement. In addition the a flank march to the Manuel Nunnery and the redeployment

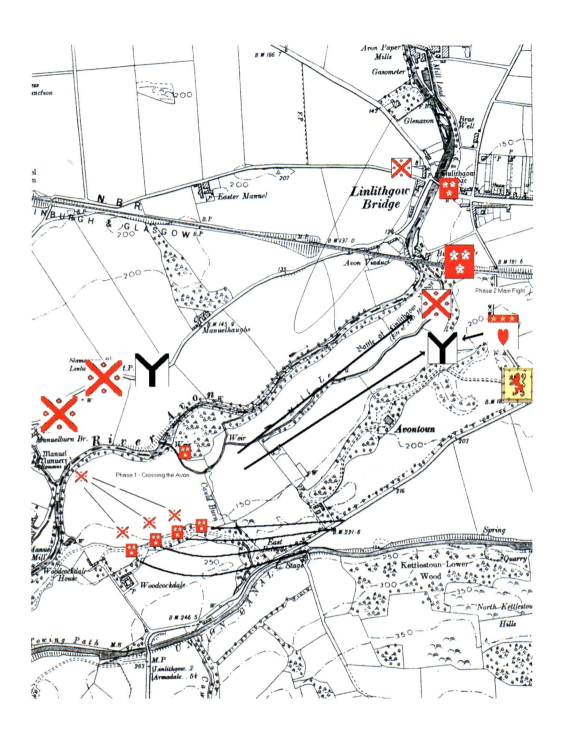

Battle Theory 1 This late 19th Century OS map shows the original location of the battlefield and the major features that dominate the landscape today but does not include the new housing and quarry works. Lennox artillery gives covering fire at the bridge whilst the main body of troops flank march to the Manuel Convent. They cross, dispersing the Hamilton skirmishes, form up in the valley plain, advance North East to face the Hamilton and Douglas troops arrayed on Pace Hill. (By Author)

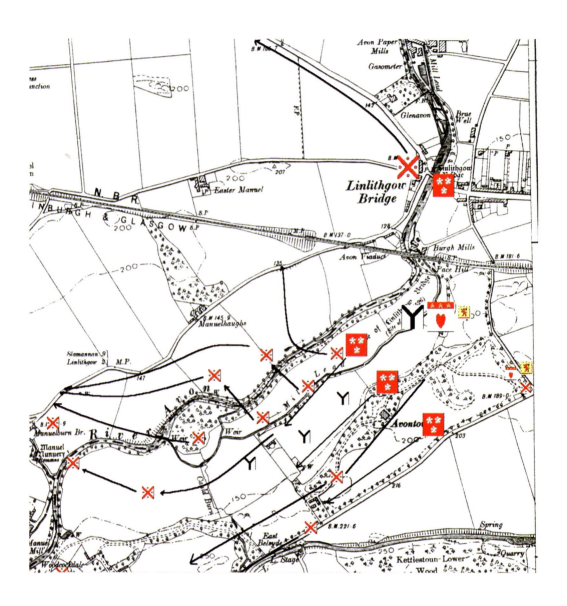

Rout TThis map shows the likely passages of rout for the Lennox forces. Hemmed in by the river and the ridge line, fleeing troops would have headed back the sanctuary of the Nunnery. (By Author)

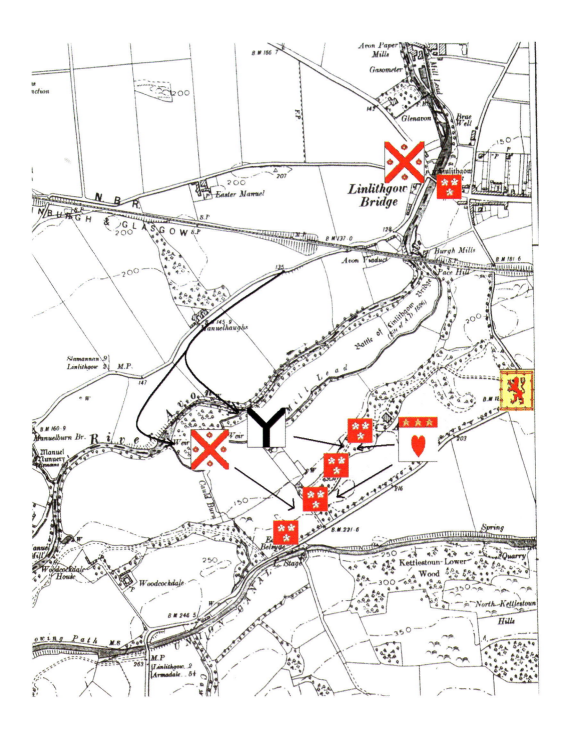

Battle theory 2 More modern accounts suggest the main fighting took place at the crossing on the plains opposite Manuel Nunnery. This suggests the Hamiltons left Pace Hill and established a defensive position along the ridge line. The Douglas reinforcements most likely advanced along the Torphichen Road. However this position would have been easily flanked and thinly manned. It was not as strong a position as that on Pace Hill. (By Author)

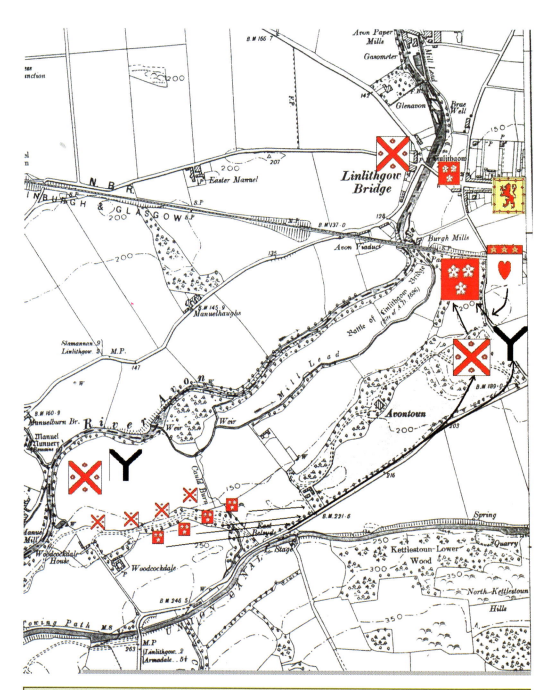

Battle Theory 3 A third theory suggests that Lennox cleared the ford of Hamilton skirmishers before climbing up onto the ridge and advancing along what Buchanan described as a 'rugged road', in this case the Torphichen Road. This brought Lennox out at the south of Pace Hill facing a lesser slope but still being overlooked by the Hamilton forces. Douglas's late advance from the West Port would have out flanked the Lennox attack and certainly been a devastating blow. However, Buchanan's account varies according to which translation you read and has been simply interpreted as Lennox was hindered by the 'difficult terrain' which suggests an advance along the flooded valley floor. (By The Author)

Manuel Convent All that remains of Manuel Convent is half the gable end. The rest was lost in the floods of the River Avon. (Authors Collection)

Haining Castle The remains of Haining Castle now lie in ruins within the bounds of an industrial park but it was most likely used by the Hamiltons as lookout and then by Lennox to hold his council of war before the battle. (Authors Collection)

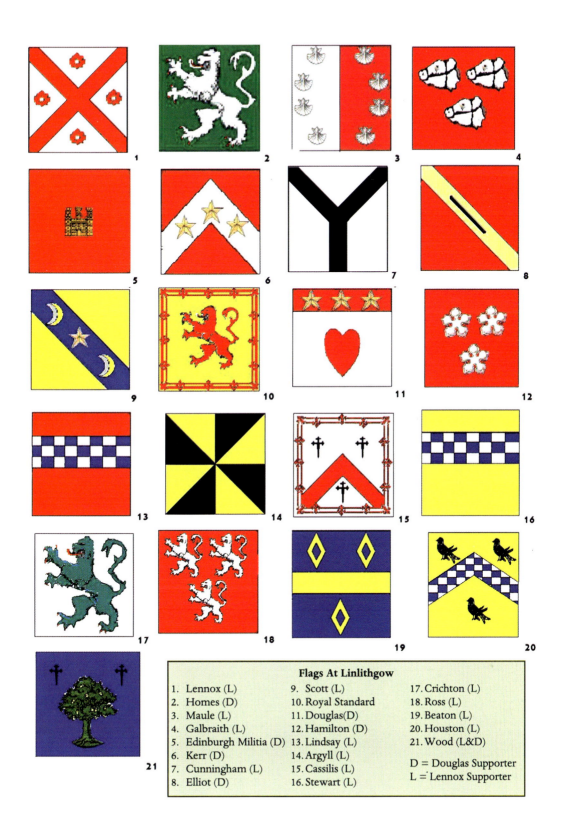

Flags At Linlithgow

1. Lennox (L)
2. Homes (D)
3. Maule (L)
4. Galbraith (L)
5. Edinburgh Militia (D)
6. Kerr (D)
7. Cunningham (L)
8. Elliot (D)
9. Scott (L)
10. Royal Standard
11. Douglas(D)
12. Hamilton (D)
13. Lindsay (L)
14. Argyll (L)
15. Cassilis (L)
16. Stewart (L)
17. Crichton (L)
18. Ross (L)
19. Beaton (L)
20. Houston (L)
21. Wood (L&D)

D = Douglas Supporter
L = Lennox Supporter

The Siege of Tantallon 1528 James V led his forces in pursuit of Douglas in 1528. The Douglases held out at Tantallon Castle but were forced into exile soon afterwards. This modern illustration accurately portrays the arms and equipment of the period. (Reproduced by kind permission of Historic Scotland.)

Advance from Crammond to Linlithgow Adair's map of 1684 shows the main routes from the River Almond to Linlithgow via Dundas Castle, Philipstoun, Pardovan and Magdalene Park or Niddry Castle, Miltoun and Kingscavil. Either way would be a good 9 hour march from Edinburgh Castle for the Douglas reinforcements (Reproduced by permission of the Trustees of the National Library of Scotland)

on the other bank would have taken between one to two more hours, forcing Lennox to start the assault of the heights very late in the day.

Clearly Lennox must have been on the move the previous day leaving him in striking distance of Linlithgow on the 4th September. The written evidence to this lies within Douglas's letter to Wolsey sent on 16th September which states:

'On the third they moved thence to Linlithgow, on their way to Edinburgh to take the King'.[84]

This makes much more sense with Lennox covering the majority of the distance on the 3rd, getting word of Hamilton's defences and deciding to save his troops for the next day's fighting. How far they made that day and where they camped overnight is not known and it is therefore uncertain as to when Lennox got to the bridge on the 4th.

Angus's arrival on the field with the Humes and the Kerrs is a little more definitive. He left to join Arran early in the morning after leaving the King and George Douglas to raise the Edinburgh militia. Angus would have needed to cover 18 miles from Edinburgh to Linlithgow at about 2 miles an hour.[85] This would mean he could reach the field in 9 hours at about 3.00 pm. Buchanan, like Drummond, states that :

'and when they [Lennox's men] had just reached the enemy, a shout announced the arrival of Douglas, who rushing from the road into the midst of the battle, quickly decided the fortune of the day'[86]

However, Pitscottie infers Douglas arrives before the fighting begins and requests the King makes haste as:

'schawand the king that baitht the airmeis was in sight of wther and was porpossit to fight,[87]

Which account is the most accurate is difficult to say and perhaps we should settle with the conclusion that Arran started the fight and Angus finished it

In the meantime George Douglas and the reluctant King were to cover the 18 miles from Edinburgh Castle to Linlithgow collecting men on the way.

The King is still in Edinburgh when:

' Be this the worde come to the toune of Edinburgh that the Earle of Lennox was within ane myle to Lythgow...[88]

Pitscottie and Leslie make great play of the delaying action James exercised, and suggests they began mustering troops after hearing of Lennox's departure from Stirling. Men were to be called up from all over Edinburgh:

'Sa schone as the Earl of Angus knew of thair coming he went and schew the king the maner how it stude, desyrand his grace gar mak procliematioun baitht in Leyht and Edinburgh that all maner of

man betuix sextie and sexten zeris sould ryse incontienent to follow the king and debait his grace.[89]

But the King was not complying with his guardian's wishes:

'The earle seand that the king was slawe in the matter wist weill thair was nathing bot ether do or die and thaifor maid him mainfullie to the fieldis and caussit his freind Archibald Douglas, provost of Edinburgh to ring the common bell and put the toun in order'[90]

Assuming the King was not ready to move until midday, this would have left him a 9 hour march before entering the fight. We know he arrived too late to have any great effect so this would mean the battle was all but over around 9.00 pm when night fell. But his aid, Andrew Wood was sent ahead on horseback and arrived in time to witness the final stand of Glencairn.

When we compare this with other engagements we can come up with some idea of the duration of the action; Pinkie took approximately 3 hours[91] and Flodden some 2-3 hours . The action at Linlithgow could have realistically expected to last no more than 3 hours. Therefore with Lennox's march in the morning and the arrival of Douglas mid way through it is likely that the battle was fast and furious and fought between 4 pm and 7 pm.

80 The Historie and Cronicles Of Scotland - Vol 2" by Robert Lindsay of Pitscottie trans JG Mackay (Scottish Text Society 1899 - 1911)

81 'History of Scotland from the year 1423 until the year 1542' by William Drummond of Hawthornden (London Edn 1681)

82 The Historie and Cronicles Of Scotland - Vol 2" by Robert Lindsay of Pitscottie trans JG Mackay (Scottish Text Society 1899 - 1911)

83 Buchanan supports this by saying that the Hamiltons had intelligence that 'John [Lennox] would march out of Stirling on that day and very early in the morning' - "The History of Scotland" - by George Buchanan trans J Aikman (Glasgow and Edinburgh 1827 - 29) vol ii

84 Calender of Letters and State Papers Henry VIII No.2487

85 Unburdened by artillery and mainly mounted it is feasible that he made better time.

86 "The History of Scotland" - George Buchanan trans J Aikman (Glasgow and Edinburgh 1827 - 29) vol ii

87 The Historie and Cronicles Of Scotland - Vol 2" by Robert Lindsay of Pitscottie trans JG Mackay (Scottish Text Society 1899 - 1911)

88 The Historie and Cronicles Of Scotland - Vol 2" by Robert Lindsay of Pitscottie trans JG Mackay (Scottish Text Society 1899 - 1911)

89 The Historie and Cronicles Of Scotland - Vol 2" by Robert Lindsay of Pitscottie trans JG Mackay (Scottish Text Society 1899 - 1911)

90 The Historie and Cronicles Of Scotland - Vol 2" by Robert Lindsay of Pitscottie trans JG Mackay (Scottish Text Society 1899 - 1911)

91 DH Caldwell's account of the Battle of Pinkie in 'Scotland and War' by Macdougall (Edinburgh : John Donald, 1991)P. 87 - 90

92 Flodden by Neill Barr quotes accounts of the battle of Flodden ed by Henry James 1865 as starting between 4 and 5 and finishing at 7.00 pm - 'Flodden, 1513' Niall Barr (Tempus 2001)

Chapter 16
'Joyned and Fightand Furiously'
The Battle of Linlithgow Bridge[93]

On the 3rd September Arran mustered his troops on the Peel at the Palace. It was estimated that he had about 2000 troops raised from the local families, all probably Hamilton supporters or kinfolk. In 1526 all the main estates around the town were owned or aligned by marriage to the Hamilton family and now by duty and family loyalty many found themselves amongst friends at the muster or 'wapinschaw'. With Lennox mustering at Stirling and the promise of reinforcements from Angus, Arran had a difficult decision to make. Perhaps remembering the events of the previous winter's bloodless defeat, Arran made the decision to stand his ground with the greatest show of force he could muster. All that day the guildsman and trade folk of the town toiled hard to prepare an impressive defence of the bridge. The final act of the evening would have been to dig in the gun platforms and bring up the ammunition for his artillery, hauled up earlier that day from Linlithgow Palace and Blackness Castle.

Leslie makes reference to Arran's preparations. Leslie states

' Arran in haist was radie , suner nor men beleuiet: and with greta power in Lythquow was present of September 3rd'[94]

Leslie goes on to describe a communication between Arran and Lennox, presumably by runner in which Arran tries to ward off the coming battle:

'Bydeng heir a lytle, he sendis to Lennox, and prays him to desist, gif he refuse, he wil nocht esteem him his sister sone bot his enimie and enimie to the Realme'[95]

Arran may have meant this concealed threat, but more likely he was playing for time. Lennox's response was not surprising, sending word that he would rescue the King or die in the attempt. This posturing could only be expected as both sides tested the resolve and loyalty of the opposition. The consequence of a full blooded battle was not to be taken lightly and here we have two protagonists giving each a final chance to back down and perhaps change sides.

By midday on the 4th the posturing was over. Arran had deployed his troops on the east side of the Avon with the artillery covering the approaches and a guard at the bridge. Despite having a day to position his guns and choose his ground, he would not have been able to site his artillery to cover much further along the Falkirk road than the crest below East Manuel Farm. However his scouts and spies would have returned with news of Lennox's approach heralded by the sound of sporadic gunfire as the covering cavalry units took pot shots at each other. It is likely Haining Castle housed Arran's pickets; however they would have put up little opposition as Lennox's horsemen arrived

It is difficult to guess the reception troops from either camp would have received from the Crawfords' of Haining. In June, Archibald Crawford of Haining had been condemned as a rebel after being implicated in the murder of Edward Cunningham of Auchinhervy, in conjunction with Hugh Montgomery Earl Of Eglington, Archibald Montgomery Master of Eglington and others relatives. Eglington was now aligned with Lennox, but the Crawfords may have felt obliged to rein in their enthusiasm to the rebellion because their neighbours the Hamiltons were just across the water in the next parish.

We can only surmise that the household looked after its own that day offering shelter for Arran's scouts on the 3rd (the view from the tower would have been manna from heaven for any decent picket commander) before opening the doors as Lennox's army approached. Whatever their politics, the castle and the Crawford family seemed to survive the day intact.

At some point Lennox rode forward to verify the reports from his cavalry scouts before sitting down with Glencairn and the Laird of Kilmaurus to come up with the decision to flank Arran's position. As Haining sits near the hamlet of Whitecross and the road down to Manuel Convent, it would have been natural for him to hold his conference of war at or near the castle.

But why the decision to bypass the bridge? Lennox knew of Arran's intention the previous day. He had already been threatened with force if he proceeded so he was aware of the probability of meeting some form of opposition. His sympathisers in the area brought him news of the fortification of the bridge and numbers of troops gathering on the Peel. He would also have been aware of the approach of reinforcements out of Edinburgh, most likely through word sent from the King himself. So he needed to act decisively and destroy the opposition in piecemeal. A frontal attack across a river, then up hill against a prepared position would have cost him dear. Even if he had carried the day it would have so weakened his army that he would have been in a poor position to take on any Douglas reinforcements. Arran's preparations had at least succeeded in slowing Lennox up and making him think again.

Lennox needed to move quickly and he had very little choice in options. Forcing a crossing down stream meant being hemmed in against Linlithgow Loch and the Binns even if he could find a place to cross. Upstream beyond Manuel was the Avon gorge. Any route taken beyond that would take him miles out of the way towards Bathgate beyond the Riccarton Hills. He would then have Arran's men threatening his rear and cutting off his line of retreat to Stirling. By then his scouts identified the Nunnery as good a place to cross as any. Whether they also told him of the state of the land on the other side of the Avon or whether he chose to ignore them, we will never know.

Blackness Castle Blackness Castle on the shores of the Firth of Forth was destined to be James's unsinkable arsenal. At the time of the battle it housed royal artillery which were available to Douglas. (Author's Collection)

Pace Hill from Manuel Hill From this position Lennox could view the artillery positions overlooking the bridge and Hamilton troops on Pace Hill, marked by a clump of trees amongst the houses in the mid right. (Authors Collection)

With time ticking by, Lennox gave his orders for the move to the ford. It is likely that he would have set up artillery pieces on Manuel Hill to cover his movement and to worry Arran's forces, although there is no mention of the resultant artillery duel in contemporary accounts. However the finds of cannon balls along the river at the Burgh Mills suggest the exchange did take place.

Lennox's men pulled their guns from the overnight bivouac and had now to deploy under the watchful gaze of their counterparts. Unlashing the draft animals, the men, now stripped down to their shirts and hose, hauled the guns down beyond the crest of the hill and into the range of the enemy gunners. The sporadic gunfire from across the river was more of an annoyance than a withering fire but with the mass of men milling around the brow of the hill it meant some were being ripped apart by passing shot. Wounded draft animals, panicked by the fire, added to the confusion. Wagons and carts were warily brought forward to unload the powder kegs and shot. Water barrels were rolled towards the thirsty guns. Mops, rams, buckets, and all the paraphernalia of the gunners' trade were brought forward from comparative safety beyond the crest. Unlike their opposition the Lennox guns were to be fired from unprepared positions and would dig into the earth under the recoil. Ropes shovels and levers would be required to reposition the bigger guns after each firing. French and Italian artillerists barked out their instructions, peered along the barrels of the guns and set their plumb lines to assess elevation. Their gun teams, some veterans of Flodden but many more new to the trade, struggled hard to interpret their commands and understand the workings of the equipment. Eventually after much effort the Lennox guns began to reply to their antagonists.

The Hamilton artillerists, already working their guns hard, were protected by a fosse and braye and earth filled gambesons and were now hidden under a pall of acrid gunsmoke. A fluttering banner of the Hamiltons broke through the haze. Bigger guns than their opponents, these pieces had been mounted on a platform of wooden planking, capable of withstanding the force of the recoil and facilitating the repositioning of the piece once reloaded. The day before had been spent sighting the guns and working out the elevations and measures of powder to land the shot at set ranges and targets. And now all the hard work was paying dividends as they ranged in on their counterparts' guns on the slopes opposite. The outcome of this personal duel would not affect the outcome of the day but would cover the battlefield with a layer of smoke and create a backdrop of the roar of gunfire. The artillery duel was heard as far away as Costorphine. The death toll minimal but bloody.

In between the two sets of guns cowered 200 Hamiltons sent to guard the bridge. A mixture of gunners, swords and buckler and a light cavalry picket, these men manned the temporary barricade on the bridge. They had, until Lennox's arrival, sent pickets along the road to Polmont and up to Haining. With artillery shot flying over their heads this tiny force came under sporadic fire from Glencairn's cavalry as they looked for alternative crossing points. As Lennox moved his men south this opposition swelled in an attempt to cover the flank march, distract Arran's attention and perhaps force a passage at the earliest opportunity. Riding hard into pistol range the cavalry would discharge their pieces into the defenders of the barricade before wheeling away to reload and seek the shelter of the far bank. The defenders however had the advantage of laying their weapons across the barricade for greater accuracy, concentrating their fire along the approach to the bridge and ducking down to reload. This skirmish would also carry on for the rest of the day, before the Lennox men got news of the defeat of the main force and melted away towards Polmont.

Despite the build up of activity at the bridge, Arran was not pinned to his position overlooking the bridge. With forces to his front and a flanking movement underway Arran had three choices. He could withdraw back through the town; this would have been a tricky move in any circumstance but it would mean many of his men could return to their homes to ensure their families were protected. He could re-deploy along the bluffs spreading his men out and forming a skirmishing line. Or he could maintain his cohesion, minimise his redeployment, turn to face south and prepare for Lennox's attack. Lennox could never leave a force the size of Arran's to his flank and rear, especially when Angus's reinforcements would confront him sooner or later along the road to Edinburgh. Arran's decision would have been made easier as soon as word of Angus's arrival came through. By facing south Arran's troops formed to the right of his ally, leaving enough space along the ridge from which all could benefit. However, even with the new troops they were still outnumbered nearly three to one. Their only hope was to hold the ridge and pray that the Edinburgh militia, and perhaps more importantly the King's standard, would arrive in time.

The Quarry The view from Pace Hill looking along the valley floor. Lennox's men would have advanced along the flood plain now quarried out and replaced by a lagoon. Unfortunately any battlefield archaeology has probably been lost in the process. (Authors Collection)

It is likely that Arran's redeployment was not spotted by Lennox who was by now a mile upstream, in the lightly wooded valley. It would have not however put him off. He had to strike and strike fast. The die was cast.

The Vanguard, consisting of the Laird of Kilmaurus' horsemen and then perhaps another 2,000 foot soldiers, made for the ford and came under heavy fire from the heights opposite the Nunnery and skirmishers around the crossing. As ball and shot whistled in, many of the horseman were knocked out of their saddles or lost control of their mounts. The remaining foot by sheer weight of numbers drove down past the Nunnery and into the waters of the Avon. Scrambling up the far bank they became a rabble, losing all shape and coherence in the ranks. With the dead and dying littering the riverbed and the walking wounded making their way back the sanctuary of the Nunnery, the remaining troops had enough momentum to cross the water meadow and storm the heights. Spent and exhausted with the action the Vanguard ceased to be. The survivors awaited Lennox.

Lennox's main battle was not long arriving, but crossing the stream and forming up was to be time consuming. Splashing through the shallows and shrinking from the sight of the horrendous wounds of the poor unfortunates around them the Highlanders and West Men shuffled into position. They dropped their haversacks, bed rolls and water flasks, took last swigs of whisky and water, and fell to their knees for their last communion. Noblemen adjusted their armour, the pages pulled tight their masters' harness straps, closed the visors on their helms and handed them their swords, before looking to their own well being. Flags were unfurled, horses and grooms despatched to the rear and final orders given. All to the sound of the occasional skirmish shot and the ranging cannon fire.

Time ticked on. Time Lennox couldn't afford to waste. At Linlithgow, as wc have already seen at Flodden, the troop's lack of experience, constant harassment from the surrounding bluffs and the marshy ground made deploying the battles a major problem.

The battles deployed with the standards at the centre surrounded by a 'guard' armed with polearms, bills and halberds. Around them stood the pike, up to 20 to 30 ranks deep. The lairds and nobles gathered their professional and most loyal household troops to the front ranks. The rest of the levy grouped around this central block. Finally to the flanks and in front, a screen of harquebusiers and bowmen mustered, preparing their weapons, stringing their bows and lighting their matches. The light field artillery were pulled through the mud in between the two battles. Despite the confusion, Arran's and Angus's men must have looked down on the spectacular sight with trepidation. The crack of guns and the artillery was complimented by the sounds of pipes, drums, fifes and trumpets. The sergeants barking out their orders, troops being fired up with song, rousing speeches and spontaneous cheering all adding to the din of an army girding its loins for the fight ahead. Eventually, to the beat of the drums, the two massive human steamrollers lurched into step, wading through the marshy ground, splashing through the shallows and stumbling across the sodden ditches.

With Lennox and Glencairn heading their respective columns there was little opportunity to redress ranks, change direction or alter the line of advance. They may not have even been aware of the slow loss of cohesion as men struggled to keep up, their pikes clattering against their neighbours and the armour seeming heavier by the step. As the first ranks approached the base of Peace Hill the concentration of fire directed against them increased and their own skirmish screens faded away from in front of them exposing the massed ranks to a hail of shot and arrow.

Buchanan goes as far as to suggest they faced a more unusual offensive:

'The Lennoxians made their way towards their enemies, but they were much inspected by abundance of stones which were rolled down from the hills upon them'[6]

The first casualties fell and rolled down the slope under the feet of those behind, the abandoned pikes forming a weave of flotsam. Negotiating this would have been similar to walking up a grease covered cattle grid.

As the casualties mounted in the front ranks the back ranks were oblivious to the fate of their colleagues. Hunkering down for protection from the incoming missiles, concentrating on keeping their weapons vertical and where they were putting their feet, they pressed on, pushing against the man in front hoping to engage with the enemy. For those in the middle, pushed from behind and obstructed by the mounting carnage ahead, it must have been intolerable. Contemporary accounts of such actions suggest men could suffocate standing up in such a press.

Finally Arran's men threw themselves down the slope into the fray. With pikes and bills levelled at the faces of the poor unfortunates on the opposing front rank, they had the momentum to cause shocking injuries and more importantly, arrest the momentum of the attack. Once stationary on the slope, you can imagine the fear. Pitscottie describes the messengers reporting the combatants as being:

'Joyned and fightand furiously' and 'yocked togidder'[7]

inferring in a few words the terrible close quarter struggle going on. Once in contact the pike became an encumbrance and many men resorted to their side arms, using stilleto blades to pierce the vulnerable areas of the armour; the eye slits, throat, armpits and groins. The final resort was to punch, scratch and gouge at their opponents with bare hands.

On the fringe of these masses there was a breathing space, room to wield a sword or fire off their 'gyns' at point blank range. The fighting here was at its most dynamic as men could move, deliver crushing blows and duck out of the way of retaliatory strikes. The maimed crawled out into this area, if they could move at all, looking for a chance to retire or offer their surrender. The rear ranks pushed on in a state of confusion. With their leaders ahead of them and the momentum lost, they did not know what to do. Then as the wounded pushed their way to the rear the back ranks opened up to let them through, losing formation, losing touch with their neighbour and finally losing heart and confidence. They looked to sneak away or perhaps 'aid' wounded colleagues to the rear. The crowd took on the state of a crumbling sandcastle in the tide, collapsing slowly around the extremities and leaving a compact mass of dead and dying at the centre

From our time line and the accounts we know this push of pike lasted for a couple of hours and was a bitterly fought contest. Modern day re-enactors soon discover that you cannot continually fight for more than ten minutes without needing to break off to rest and take water. You tend to discard unnecessary weapons and clothing leaving the field strewn with equipment. Broken kit can be replaced or repaired, minor wounds treated and essential armour secured. It is at these times when you can take stock, plan your next move or question your resolve to continue.

In the centre of the crush this 'stop-start' was impossible to initiate but at the peripheries where there was space, bodies of men dropped back for rest, sometimes being replaced in the line, sometimes instigating a standoff. This may have been for minutes or perhaps for longer, invariably flaring up again as casualties mounted from bow and shot. Or, once rested, driven by the want to settle old scores, loyalty to reckless lairds or perhaps driven insane by post stress disorder, men threw themselves into the fray again. The front ranks crashed together, broke away and surged forward again.

The role of the commanders at this point was limited. Leading from the front ranks, inspiring only the handful of people immediately around them they had little sway on the outcome of the fight. Arran and Angus may have had a better view of the fight as they held higher ground, but the clamour and noise of battle made communication between them almost impossible. Of more influence were the standards of the families. Their position and movement for many was the only indication of the state of the proceedings. Although not recorded for this battle there are many accounts of the casualties sustained in fighting to defend or take flags.[98] To see the standard fall, and not the commander, would have been for many the clearest indication of the battles progress and the catalyst for the retreat.

The 'whifflers' and sergeants, like in so many conflicts throughout history, were the key to the local tactical fighting. They asserted control by cajoling, inspiring, threatening and at times resorting to physical violence against their own. As respected members of the home towns or paid professionals from the wars in Europe, these men held together pockets of resistance, linking one section of the battle line to the next. As they were lost so would be the coherence of the masses.

Finally with the fainthearted and wounded fading away and the corpses mounting along the heights and at the foot of the slope, the momentum was lost and Arran's men were left still holding the ridge. Lennox's attacks petered out. The crush of pike lessened and dissolved into pockets of resistance, retinues grouping around their leaders or more likely the banners. What made these men stand to the end can only be wondered at. Facing death but not wanting to flee, pulled together by kinship, loyalty and pride, these knots of men stood together alone.

Again we can return to Pitscottie's account of Glencairn's desperate stand and read it in context of the final fighting:

> ' Earle of Glencairne still fightand witht thirty men leift of all his airmie on lyue unskaine and fled frome him, bot zeit was in sic ane strength that his enemies might on nawayis wa him sa lang as he had ony men left on lyue to defend him.'[99]

There reaches a point in every conflict where one side breaks, sometimes on command but more likely as their resolve to fight fades away. It is impossible to say when Lennox's men reached this point. Most likely this was at the arrival of Angus's main force, but we know it was before the king's arrival. The steady flow of refugees became a flood, funnelled back down the way they had come, then at a safe point re-crossing the river or carrying on to Bathgate on the east bank. Wounded sought sanctuary at the Nunnery and surrounding buildings, the nuns caring for as many as they could, or making their way to family friends or kinfolk in the surrounding district. Pitscottie alludes to a bloody retreat when describing James Hamilton as leaving:

> 'all that he might owertak that day witht his mark'[100]

suggesting at least some sort of pursuit took place. Buchanan also relates a pursuit in which:

> ' The Hamiltonians used their victory with a great deal of cruelty.'[101]

We can perhaps envisage scenes similar to those described in the graphic accounts of the rout from Pinkie. Patten's 'The Expedicion into Scotland of Edward, Duke of Somerset 1548' describes the retreat at Pinkie vividly:

> ' some to stay in the river, covering down his body, his head under the root of a willow tree, with scant his nose above the water for breath' and 'others again for their more lightness, cast away shoes and doublets; and ran in their shirts. And some were seen in the race to fall flat down all breathless, and to have run themselves to death'[102]

- an account which could have easily described the rout after Linlithgow Bridge. But as the victorious troops had been seriously tested, taken many casualties and outnumbered almost 3 to 1, we can assume the pursuit was limited by fatigue and the onset of darkness.

It is at this point that Pitscottie and Buchanan describe the frantic search by Andrew Wood of Largo for survivors and the death of Lennox. Pitscottie as a chronicler cannot always be trusted, as he tends to exaggerate the more romantic aspects especially when other contemporaries make no reference to the event. Certainly John Leslie makes no reference to the murder of Lennox. Pitscottie states that Andrew Wood was despatched with a number of the kings trusted men to ride ahead of the approaching Edinburgh militia and attempt to:

' stanche the slaughter, and in spetiall to saif the Earle of Lennox gif he could be comprehendit allyue {alive}.'[103]

Wood spurred his horse on, and followed by his small band of horseman made for the field. He would have galloped down the High Street of Linlithgow, making his way through the crowds of onlookers, wounded and stragglers, following the sounds of battle. On reaching the West Port he most probably turned south west along the Torphichen Road (now the A706) and come out at the left flank of Angus's men. Here he found the murdered body of Lennox.

93   It was not until the Ordnanace Surveys of the 18th Century did this battle take the name of Linlithgow Bridge, being referred to as the action at the bridge across the Avon. Linlithgow Bridge as a community did not exist at the time of the battle

94   The Historie Of Scotland - Vol 2" by Jhone Leslie Ed Thomas Thomson (Bannatyne Club 1830)

95   The Historie Of Scotland - Vol 2" by Jhone Leslie Ed Thomas Thomson (Bannatyne Club 1830)

96   "The History of Scotland" - George Buchanan trans J Aikman (Glasgow and Edinburgh 1827 - 29) vol ii

97   The Historie and Cronicles Of Scotland - Vol 2" by Robert Lindsay of Pitscottie trans JG Mackay (Scottish Text Society 1899 - 1911)

98   The Trewe Encountre, a contemporary account of the Battle of Flodden for example makes great account of Edmund Howard's plight early on in the fight and states 'his standarde and berer of the same betten and hewed to peces'. A common fate for many a standard bearer that day.

99   The Historie and Cronicles Of Scotland - Vol 2" by Robert Lindsay of Pitscottie trans JG Mackay (Scottish Text Society 1899 - 1911)

100   The Historie and Cronicles Of Scotland - Vol 2" by Robert Lindsay of Pitscottie trans JG Mackay (Scottish Text Society 1899 - 1911)

101   "The History of Scotland" - George Buchanan trans J Aikman (Glasgow and Edinburgh 1827 - 29) vol ii

102   Patten's 'The Expecdicion into Scotland of Edward, Duke of Somerset 1548'

103   The Historie and Cronicles Of Scotland - Vol 2" by Robert Lindsay of Pitscottie trans JG Mackay (Scottish Text Society 1899 - 1911)

Chapter 17
'The Stoutest Man, the Hardiest Man'
The Death of Lennox

The accepted account and the one that Pitscottie describes in great detail, is that Lennox is wounded in the fight but is able to surrender his sword to the Laird Of Pardovan, William Hamilton. However much against the chivalry of the time Sir James Hamilton of Finnart (the same man who instigated the fighting in Edinburgh 6 years earlier) steps forward and:

'gart schut him fre his takoris and thair slew him without marcie'[104]

Certainly this would not have been beyond the character of the man, but we must remember Pitscottie wrote in hindsight after James Hamilton had been burnt at the stake for treason in 1540. Perhaps Pitscottie totally exaggerated the event in an attempt to justify the recent verdict. The English court was under the impression that Lennox had been murdered as little as 2 years later. Sir Thomas Magnus during negotiations of the peace treaty in 1528 declared that Henry could never deal with a king who looked to;

'theves and murderous' amongst them 'Sir James Hamyltoun, whoe did sley the Erle of Lenneux'.[105]

Whatever the facts of the death, the murder of Lennox has been placed firmly into local folk law and was enough to see Finnart executed.[106]

The cairn today provides us with a mystery in itself. It stands some three feet high, made of neatly hewn stone and has a centre piece of two somewhat older looking plaques. The top bears the remains of a plaque bearing the number 628. The bottom is inscribed with the fading outline of what can only be described as a child's representation of a house with a 'rose' motif where the front door should be, described by local historians as the Lennox coat of arms. It is located somewhat conveniently at the entrance of a modern housing estate. It all seems too good to be true.

In fact the original inscribed blocks have had a more complicated history than you might expect. The maps of 1856 clearly sites the cairn in or around the area now occupied by houses on the Kettlestoun Mains estate. Reference is made in the Statistical Account of Scotland 1795 to the fact that the cairn is

'one of those rude memorials to which passengers often added a stone"[107]

suggesting it bore no inscription or motifs

Locals recall yearly gatherings of presumably Stewart Clan members at the cairn, which was positioned on a grassy mound in one of the farm's fields. However the owners of Kettlestoun Farm required a ready source of masonry to build up a retaining wall in the farm complex and recycled the cairn for the purpose. Eventually, when the farm was due to be demolished to make way for the housing estate, local historians rescued the remaining stonework and had it remounted in its present location some 50yds from it original site[108] It is therefore safe to say that the cairn marks the approximate location of the event. It also provides the approximate location of an area of the battlefield considered safe to accept the surrender of the rebel leader, presumably immediately behind the Douglas lines near the end of the battle.

Lennox 's body was also visited by Arran who is said to have covered the body with his cloak. Perhaps Lennox's best epitaph was, according to Pitscottie, Arran's declaration:

' *"the stoutest man the hardiest man that ewer was brede in Scotland was slaine that day"'* [109]

With Lennox dead, Wood continues on his search and looking down into the river plain would have picked out the standard of Glencairn and the remaining survivors of his retinue. Pitscottie writes:

'Bot imedeatlie Andrew Wode the Kingis serwand tuik him and saiffit him and brocht him away on lyue and conwoyit him to ane quyit place quhair nether the Douglassis nor the Hamilltounis might comprehend him to do him skaitht"[110]

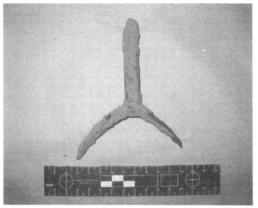

Cross and Spur These very personal articles were found on Manuel Hill and may have been lost during the battle. (Authors Collection)

Many of the Queen's men were not that lucky. We have no account of the exact number of casualties but again Pitscottie poetically alludes to a great slaughter:

'this matter beand finischit and money slaine and taine on baitht the sydis and in spetiall the earle of lennox witht money gentillmen of the wast land witht him and in lyke wyse the Earle of Glencairne ewil wondit to the deid and money of his freindis and serwandis slaine and also sum gentillmen of Fyfe baitht taine and slaine to wit, the Laird of Lethine[111] slaine witht money wther gentillmen taine"[112]

Leslie adds another Laird to the casualty list:

'heir specialis ar slane the Erle of Lennox self, and the Laird of Houstoun, with mony ane of Lenox his parte.'[113]

On the 13th September Magnus writes to Wolseley expressing his opinion that the new alliance between Angus and Arran would only be broken by the Archbishop of St Andrews. His assumption is based on the fact that the Abbots of Melrose and Dunfermline

'breder and nephew to the sed Archbishop are slain[114] and also his friend the Lord of Keir,[115] John Stirling, Captain of Stirling and many others of his Kin."[116]

Magnus also adds that

'Jas and Will[iam] Steward brothers of Lord Avondale are both slain. They were special servants to the Queen and brothers to Harry Stewarde who attends her grace"[117]

There is no mention of any high ranking casualties amongst the Hamilton or Douglas dead.

Extrapolating the death toll at Linlithgow from Flodden (5000 dead out of 20000) and Pinkie (6000 out of 23000 suggested by Earl of Huntly) would place the number at around 25% of the defeated force. Often the casualties on the winning side are much smaller in comparison as much of the killing is carried out in the rout. That gives us a figure of 3000 to 4000 Lennoxonians with around 500 to 1000 falling for the Douglas cause.

There are a number of local recollections of grave pits and human remains being found in the vicinity. We have already mentioned the building work around Justinhaugh Drive that is said to have brought up a lot of human bones. However the best documented[118] discovery supposedly linked to the battle was that of the burials discovered when they laid the foundations to the viaduct in 1840. A number of stone slab coffins were uncovered along with bones and a selection of weapons. A basket hilted sword from the find now hangs in the local museum and is reputedly from the battle. Unfortunately there is tenuous evidence of basket hilted swords being around in the 1570's[119] but it would be stretching it to believe that this was wielded at the battle some 50 years earlier. It is also unlikely that a casualty of the battle would have been laid to rest in such a dignified manner and even more unlikely that he would have been allowed to keep his sword especially if he was on the losing side. This particular soldier was most likely not a casualty of this action and more likely of Jacobean origins.

Similar stone slabbed coffins were uncovered in the excavations at the south end of the recreation ground for the housing estates around Avonmill in 1927. As they were laid East to West, the experts at the time labelled them as 'medieval'. Newspaper cuttings at the time suggest the graves were covered up and we can only assume that they still lie under somebody's house or back garden to this day.

The most likely location of any grave pits for the casualties was at the Nunnery but as most of the cemetery south of the chapel was washed away in the floods it is unlikely that the remains are around today. Otherwise grave pits may exit undiscovered.

With the battle won and the light fading, Arran and Angus returned to Linlithgow Palace to the wild applause of the local Hamiltons. Here Pitscottie and Leslie differ in their accounts.

Houston House The Sir Patrick Houston, Laird of Houston House was killed fighting for Lennox and many of his lands were subsequently lost to the Hamiltons. The house is now an excellent hotel. (Authors Collection)

Pitscottie takes great pains to mention that the Hamiltons, Douglases, Kerrs and Humes hold one of those renowned parties in the Palace, which takes most of the night, but the King, grieving for his uncle and concerned for his own position, retires early. Pitscottie describes the King as:

' *sorowful and onerous*'[120]

Leslie, on the other hand, has the King and his captors riding hard for Stirling in an attempt to capture the Queen Dowager and Beaton, only to get there and find they have gone into hiding. This is borne out by the entries in the RSS which on the 4th records four entries; two signed in Edinburgh presumably in the morning, one in Linlithgow handing over the lands of the recently deceased Patrick Houston and the last in Stirling, this time handing over Lennox estates to John Cunningham and Annabel Campbell. However, the Edinburgh entry hands over land of the '*deces of umquhile Johne Erle of Levinax*' to George Douglas which was either written after the battle, forged or the King (more likely George) was pre-empting the result.[121]

Both chroniclers go on to agree that in the following days Douglas supporters sacked Dunfermline Abbey and St Andrews Castle in the search for the Bishop. However, Beaton had taken to the hills, literally. He had disguised himself as a shepherd and was tending flocks on the Boroughmuir.

104 The Historie and Cronicles Of Scotland - Vol 2" by Robert Lindsay of Pitscottie trans JG Mackay (Scottish Text Society 1899 - 1911)
105 State Papers of Henry VIII (London 1830 - 1852) iv,pt. Iv, nocxcvii
106 Albany's memorandum to Du Prat makes no mention of the murder despite Albany's intention to drum up support against Douglas. Adam Abell's account of the battle suggests it was Angus who commited the murder.
107 'Statistical Account of Scotland 1795' by Sir John Sinclair (Wakefield EP Publishing 1979)
108 See Appendix 1 for a fuller account of this amazing investigation work and rescue
109 The Historie and Cronicles Of Scotland - Vol 2" by Robert Lindsay of Pitscottie trans JG Mackay (Scottish Text Society 1899 - 1911)
110 The Historie and Cronicles Of Scotland - Vol 2" by Robert Lindsay of Pitscottie trans JG Mackay (Scottish Text Society 1899 - 1911)
111 Mackay in translating Pitscottie suggests this is David Sibbald, Laird of Letham in Fife
112 The Historie and Cronicles Of Scotland - Vol 2" by Robert Lindsay of Pitscottie trans JG Mackay (Scottish Text Society 1899 - 1911)
113 The Historie Of Scotland - Vol 2" by Jhone Leslie Ed Thomas Thomson (Bannatyne Club 1830)
114 The Abbacy of Melrose was received from Robert Beaton by Andrew Dury in 1525, However it is most likely Robert who is killed at Linlithgow and Magnus is yet to catch up with change of job. The Abbot of Dunfermline at the time was Archbishop James Beaton having taken over from Andrew Foreman in 1522, supposedly on his death which suggests this claim is incorrect. However other sources state that it was Foreman who died at Linlithgow
115 The more recent account by Ferguson adds Stirling Of Kerr among the slain. However this could be incorrect as although he was with Lennox at the battle and had his lands taken from him as a result, he lived another 13 years before he was murdered at Stirling Bridge in revenge for his assassination of Buchanan of Leny. There may have been confusion as to who the casualty was or it was misreported.
116 State Papers Henry VIII (London 1830 - 1852) Vol iv p458
117 This is difficult to verify as the only legitimate brothers of Henry were Andrew 1st Lord of Ochiltree d 1548 and James of Beith who died 1544
118 'History of the Town and Parish of Linlithgow' by G Waldie 3rd Edition Published 1879
119 'Scottish Weapons and Fortifications 1100 - 1800' by DH Caldwell (Edinburgh John Donald 1981)
120 The Historie and Cronicles Of Scotland - Vol 2" by Robert Lindsay of Pitscottie trans JG Mackay (Scottish Text Society 1899 - 1911)
121 Another letter 3489 is listed within those written on the 4th, to Malcolm Lord Fleming, is without place, date and is incomplete suggesting James was in the process of writing this letter before being hurried out to go to Linlithgow.

Chapter 18
'This Cruell and Unhappie Feild
The Aftermath

By the end of September 1526 the King found himself very much alone. Lennox, his favoured advisor and uncle, was dead. His mother:

'gaed vagrant, disguysed a long time',[122]

Beaton was reputedly:

'turned a true Pastor and in Shepherd's weeds kept sheep upon some hill"[123]

and by the end of the year he had surrendered the Abbey of Kilwinning over to Arran, paid some 2000 Scotch marks to Angus and 1000 each to George Douglas and James Hamilton.

The lords who fought for the King's freedom were now summoned to appear before Angus to seek mercy. A letter from Sir Christopher Dacre to Lord Dacre written on the 2nd Dec 1526 sums up their plight:

'Lords Cassilis and Avondale are in the hands of Arran, and Sir James Hamilton, to ransom at their pleasure, with others of the West of the Party of Lennox, Lindsay and others of the same party are in the hands of Angus and Sir George Douglas, to whom the lands of Carr are forfeited'.[124]

Some had been more fortunate than others:

'Rynyame Creghton, who was in the keeping of Drumlarig, has agreed with him and been restored. Buckleugh is respited and was in Lithqw on Sunday to the great displeasure of the Carrs.'

The Accounts of the Lord High Treasurer details the cost of the numerous messengers sent to Earl of Cassilis and Crichton demanding their attendance at court. Many lairds forfeited their lands and rents to appease Angus. Each swore allegiance to the King and his keepers.

Angus had successfully fought in the King's defence three times and had won on each occasion. His enemies were not keen to face him a fourth time on their own. To make matters worse for James, the Earl of Cassilis, under threat of torture, handed over condemning letters detailing the King's involvement in the uprising. The King would not be allowed to coordinate such a rebellion again.

By 1527 James was called upon to face one more humiliating turn of events as his mother finally returned to Edinburgh, with Harry Stewart in tow. They were immediately besieged within the castle by Angus. James was brought to the siege lines to view his mother's capitulation and the imprisonment of her suitor at the King's pleasure. This was the final straw for James. His loathing for his mother's partner paled into insignificance against that he held for Angus. If Linlithgow had been the spark, the next few years of captivity was the fuel he needed to ignite his determination to flee from Angus.

Not that Angus treated James cruelly. Far from it; Angus surrounded by his kinfolk in court felt safe enough to pamper and appease the King. He bought him fine clothes, swords, crossbows, hand culverins and even hawks. Angus also had the King's keepers ensure he was introduced to drink, gambling and the pleasures of female company. Angus sadly neglected James's education, perhaps in an attempt to turn his thoughts to the finer pleasures in life permanently and thus distract him from interfering with Angus's future plans.

But James had learnt in captivity to bide his time. And as he waited, he brooded and his loathing increased by the day. It spilled over into his wider politics as a growing hatred of his uncle Henry, who seemed to make no effort to affect his release or help his mother. In turn this strengthened his belief in Albany and the benefits of the Auld Alliance. It was these sentiments that were to affect his policy making in the future.

But more importantly for Scotland his imprisonment and witnessing the death of so many of his closest allies at Linlithgow and Melrose turned James from a carefree child into a self centred, suspicious and uncaring teenager. He trusted nobody, looked upon every promise of support as false and developed an inner belief that he was in control of his own destiny. By 1527, Angus had reached his zenith. Linlithgow had ensured his closest rivals had been either put to the sword or brought to account for their treason. The Lords now clearly feared for their lives should they raise a hand against the Douglases. Angus held most of the major fortresses in Scotland and rested easy in the fact that Henry in England would back his every move.

But what kind of power was this? The people of Scotland still held allegiance with the King and his mother. The Lords were pacified, but very few would support him in time of trouble. Even Arran with whom he had generously shared out the Lennox estates after the battle, had now deserted him, disgusted by the manner in which the lands had been acquired. By 1528 it was all to come crashing down around Angus's ears.

The Douglases's tenuous grip on the throne was prised open as James took matters into his own hands. Angus could not expect to exert his power in all corners of the realm without the support of the lairds, but he incredibly failed to garrison Stirling, the strongest fortress outside Edinburgh. The King saw his chance and made his own arrangements with Margaret to swap Stirling for Methven near Perth on condition that on his release he would make Henry Stewart Lord Methven. Margaret agreed and Stirling once again became a royal stronghold and focal point for insurgency. James then wrote to all his supporters to meet him at the castle as soon as they heard news of his release.

Linlithgow Palace By the evening of 4th September 1526 the Palace resounded to the sound of partying as Douglas's supporters celebrated their victory. (Authors Collection)

Falkland Palace Pitscottie would have us believe James escaped the Douglases whilst on a hunting trip in 1528 to Falkland Palace In reality he most likely fled from Edinburgh. (Author's Collection)

Dunfermline Abbey Dunfermline Abbey was the first place Douglas ransacked in the aftermath of the battle in his pursuit of the Abbot James Beaton, a powerful supporter of the Queen Dowager. (Author's Collection.)

If we are to believe Pitscottie, James fled from his stepfather whilst on a hunting trip to Falkland Palace. He supposedly took advantage of his escorts making their excuses one evening and left James Douglas of Parkhead in sole charge. James made his apologies and went to bed, insisting on an early call the next day. Instead of retiring though James went to the stables, borrowed a cloak and horse and made good his escape to Stirling.

Unfortunately close examination of the Exchequer Rolls would suggest otherwise and that he actually fled from Edinburgh sometime between 28th and 30th May. It would be nice to think that James rode hard along the Stirling road through the deserted streets of Linlithgow that May evening. And perhaps he took time out on his way to stop off at the grave of his most favoured uncle, John Stewart 3rd Earl of Lennox.[125] The boy had now come of age through the sacrifice of thousands who had died in attempting to release him from the captivity. Now the sons and heirs of the lairds that had stood by his father at Flodden gathered as they had for Lennox some 22 months earlier, awaiting his arrival at Stirling. King James may have passed his complements to the dead of Linlithgow Bridge before returning to the saddle and riding hard to Stirling. By June 1528 the minority was over, James V assumed his rightful place as King of the Scots.

122 "The History of Scotland" - George Buchanan trans J Aikman (Glasgow and Edinburgh 1827 - 29) vol ii

123 The Historie and Cronicles Of Scotland - Vol 2" by Robert Lindsay of Pitscottie trans JG Mackay (Scottish Text Society 1899 - 1911)

124 Letters and Papers , Foreign and Domestic of the reign of Henry VIII (Vaduz, 1965.)

125 James's grief for his dead Uncle is vividly portrayed in the carvings that adorned the new Royal Palaces in Stirling. Two of the carvings have cherub's heads in the background which are thought to depict the fact that the subject is deceased. One of these survives only in part and depicts a young man wearing a tunic, ornamented in low relief which is heavily embroided. This is thought to be Lennox . In the background appears to be two animals in combat perhaps a reference to the battle.

Appendix 1
The History of the Cairn

I placed an article in the local paper asking for information as part of the research for this book. The result was outstanding. I was introduced to Cris Clelland , a distinguished lady now in her nineties who was happy to recount the work of her husband David Clelland.

David was a local historian and retired policeman who put his investigative nature into good use by tracking down the lost Lennox Cairn. The search for the cairn that once marked the gravesite of Lennox started when David found an OS map dated 1854. On it was clearly marked the site of the Lennox cairn situated on land adjoining Kettlestoun Farm

According to one of the press articles, Dave disputed the most popular account of the battle related in the book 'Place Names of West Lothian' by Macdonald which had suggested 'the cairn under which the dead Earl had been buried was opened and the railway line now runs through it'. Clearly the site on the OS map was nowhere near the viaduct. David suggested that the railworkers had actually discovered a mass grave from the battle and not the Earl's last resting place.

Interestingly, David goes on to tell the reader about a local called Jimmy Calder who recalled seeing people gathering around a mound near Kettlestoun Farm conducting a service of prayer. David visited the site and concluded that the cairn had been pulled down some years before the viaduct had been built and the stones put to better use. His investigation led to the farm itself where he found a stone bearing the coats of arms of the Lennox built into the wall of an outhouse.

This appears to be the end of the story. David suggested it be made into a monument to mark the spot suggested on the OS map. The farmer who owned the buildings thought otherwise and so the stone remained in place.

Dave Clelland in the vicinity of Lennox Cairn in 1977 David Clelland, an avid local historian, pictured here on the battlefield. The land is now occupied by a leisure centre. The Lennox Cairn was originally situated in the field in the background. (Cris Clelland)

Some years later the farm was deserted and plans made to build what is now the Kettlestoun estate. It was left to local historians to carry out a desperate rescue mission to retrieve the stone from the wrecking ball. They raised enough funds and interest to have the stone removed and mounted in the current location at the entrance to the new estate along with a marker stone that bears the number '628.'

So the cairn now lies approximately 100 yds south west from its original mound. But is this all that it seems? Interestingly the picture that accompanied the article in the paper appears to show the 'coat of arms' upside down to its current position. It appears in the picture as what can be best described as an upside down child's representation of a house with a spike protruding from the apex of the 'roof' pointing downwards. There is still today a moulding in the centre of the shape at what may appear as the centre of a Saltire, however it is well weathered and difficult to make out. And what of the number '628'? It is certainly not the date of the battle. In fact this is the number of the plot of land allocated to Kettlestoun Farm before its demolition and so is more a reminder of the farm rather than having any connection to the battle.

The Stewart Society has no record of the final resting place of this man. It therefore leads us to the possibility that the 'mound' visited regularly by well wishers those many years ago could have been his grave or perhaps the mass grave of many of his men. This area now lies under the bricks and mortar of the houses so perhaps we will never know.

But thanks to David and his erstwhile colleagues, we have a lasting monument, a solid, tangible memorial not only to Lennox but to all the Scots who fought and died that day.

And as a closing remark. I was told through other sources that David had left a find from the battlefield with Cris. On my second visit I asked tentatively whether she still had the artefact. Cris knew exactly where to go and pulled out of her cabinet drawer an arquebus ball that David had told her was found on the banks of the Avon down by the Burgh Mills. That was not all. Cris went to her bathroom and from the shelf got down a cannonball…as you do. Flattened on one side perhaps after impacting its target, it had been secured to the shelf by Blue Tack, as Cris ironically remarked 'so as not to hurt anyone should it roll off !'.

Appendix 2
Wargaming the Battle

This action is a classic blocking scenario perhaps more common in a Napoleonic or WWII campaign. Such holding actions were not the norm in the late middle ages where armies met at set times and prearranged locations. As such the players have an opportunity to fight a renaissance action where the final result can be undecided to the very end should the umpire be clever enough to control the arrival of the various factions. This would be particularly effective if the action is disguised as an Italian Wars scenario or the players have not read this book. The player playing Lennox can be fed all the relevant reconnaissance information for him to make his decision before the board is set out. And of course he should not be constrained to the split of his forces, perhaps preferring a bigger assault at the bridge coordinated with a smaller flanking action. Arran may also be given a free rein to move his few troops closer to the ford or let Lennox come to him.

There are numerous 'what if' scenarios to provide an interesting tactical insight into why Lennox decided on the tactics he did on the day. Consider recreating a frontal assault across the bridge against a prepared position followed by a fight against Douglas's battle; this would hopefully justify Lennox's decision not to try such an action. Likewise wargaming the scenario where Lennox's men do out flank Arran, but make for Edinburgh rather than taking the bridge

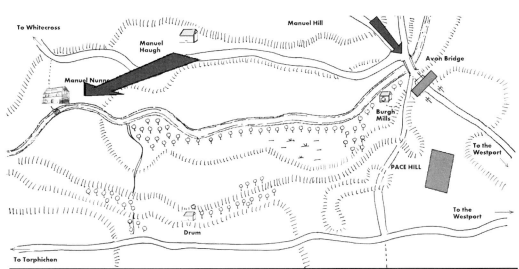

Wargame Map of Linlithgow Bridge Arran's troops can set up anywhere on Pace Hill and deploy a guard and guns at the bridge. Lennox may view their dispositions before deciding on where to launch his attack. His forces can enter from anywhere along the top edge of the board. Arran may then move to counter any threat as he sees fit. The Douglas reinforcements will arrive from the West Port. (By the Author)

and are then caught strung out in the suburbs south of Linlithgow between Arran, Angus and eventually the Edinburgh militia. This would be an interesting two front encounter similar to 2nd Newbury in the English Civil War.

We have wargamed this action on a number of occasions now in order to get a better in sight into the progress of the battle, how long the action took and the viability of the different theories on the dispositions. Lennox has failed to win on each occasion, but only just. It makes for a close, hard fought action.

If Skirmish games are more your thing then Melrose and Clense the Causey are ideal

Not much is known of the troop disposition at Melrose but here is a suggested layout.

Melrose is an ideal ambush scenario, but Buccleuch decided to present all his forces before the King hoping the impressive array would persuade Douglas to hand over his ward without a fight. Douglas responded by dismounting his force and charging the opposition. He was saved by the timely arrival of the Humes and the Kerrs. The arrival of reinforcements would best be controlled by chance cards.

Alternatively Buccleuch could be allowed to deploy ambush parties and given the victory condition of rescuing the King, could ultimately use a Lennox led retinue to try and break out of Darnock with the King, providing an interesting twist in the closing stages of the game.

Douglas excelled himself in this fight so he should be classed as an Elite character leading his small retinue of dedicated followers; Walter Scott may also be rated highly but his band of thieves and Reivers although numerous should be of poor quality. Victory points should be given to Buccleuch's men for every Laird they lure into ambush and the Douglas's should be tasked with bagging as many traitors as they can.

Clense the Causey would be an ideal project for a club presentation. The scenery itself would be a mammoth undertaking for an individual but would be a definite reward winning display game for a club. Be sure to allow the Douglases to set up their barricades and initiate the fight. Hamilton victory conditions may be simply to try to escape capture and get out of the city the best they can. Douglases are out to kill or capture as many Hamiltons as possible.

If you are looking for that award winning audience participation game, then how about Lennox's lightning raid on Holyrood? Seven unsuspecting Lennoxonians can be tasked to

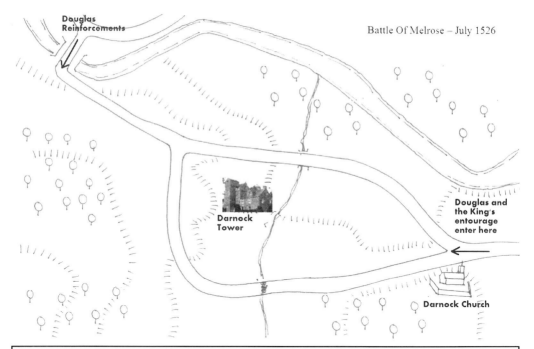

Douglas Reinforcements

Darnock Tower

Douglas and the King's entourage enter here

Darnock Church

Wargame Map of Melrose The Kings entourage will enter the board from Melrose and must make good their escape either across the bridge towards Edinburgh or back to the sanctuary of Melrose Abbey. Buccleuch's troops are free to set up ambushes with a quarter of his total force anywhere on the board with the exception of Darnock Tower itself. The rest enter the game on the left hand edge of the board. The King will move directly to Darnock Tower as soon as the trap is sprung. The relief column led by Cessford and Kerr will enter the board across the bridge. (By the Author)

negotiate the maze of corridors looking for the King and Glencairn whilst being hunted down by the Douglas supporters. Visually stunning and a fresh topic, this could be an excellent club project.

And finally for you siege buffs where else can you find an amphibious assault on a castle during the Renaissance. The assault on Wark Castle offers a very 'buildable' castle with a small yet determined garrison. The scenario has added spice by the fact that it is set in the winter snows and requires boat loads of French mercenaries crossing the swollen river as they are peppered with shot from the ramparts above. Visions of Robert Redford in the 'Bridge Too Far' come to mind.

All the actions of the minority could be pulled together into a pulsating campaign. Douglas based in Edinburgh being forced to face down a number of rescue attempts. The players launching various raids and sorties towards the capital and if they are successful having to hold onto their ward until he comes of age.

There is not a great deal of choice when it comes to appropriate figures. Most figure manufacturers concentrate on high medieval or the Italian Wars; however shopping around will enable you to build armies that have the right breakdown of troop types in suitable Scottish attire. Flodden ranges are the best starting point but at the time of writing the 28mm and 15mm choice is limited, especially if you are after a variety of figures and poses to portray the rag tag nature of the pike blocks. However Redoubt Enterprises currently provide the best variety of 25mm figures for the period by one single manufacturer

Front rank noblemen may also be few and far between but don't be afraid to convert War of the Roses Men At Arms or well armed Swiss / Flemish mercenaries. Beware the Reiver collections as these tend to be set in the later 16th century, depicting slashed baggy trousers and ruffs. They could be used at a push but the purists may mark you down. Some of the Reiver horsemen however in padded jacks are appropriate. Beware also the Highlanders in kilts, look to the Wars of Independence ranges before Jacobite to provide a suitable variety of figures. You should deploy light spearmen in aketons and T tunics rather than stooping to deploying ranks of kilted claymore and targe wielding clansmen. Early Renaissance artillery is fairly easy to source as they often portray gun crews stripped down to shirt sleeves which allows them to fit in to many armies. And of course don't forget the contingent of European mercenaries to add the touch of colour and a smattering of 'A' class resilience.

You can be reassured that purchasing appropriate figures for this conflict will not limit your choice of future battles. Not only are there plenty of scraps with the English to contemplate, Scottish troops of the period fought in Italy, Sweden and Germany.

Feel free to use the flags detailed in the colour prints. But remember to add a suitable cadency marks and bordures for kin folk. A sprinkling of banners and retinue flags derived from the heraldry of the family would also be appropriate.[126]

126 *The National Museum of Scotland has two fine examples of early 16th Century banners, one attributed to the Humes of Polwarth and the other to the Douglases of Cavers. Both may have appeared at Linlithgow.*

Appendix 3
Full version of Pitscottie

The king hierand thir wordis send for the Earle of Lennox and spak with him and gaif him commissioun to raise his leigis as he pleissit to that effect that he sould com to Edinburgh witht all the powar that he might beand tak the Kingis out of the Douglassis handis perforce. The Earle of Lennox heirand this charge and commisioun of the King was weill contentit to obey the samin and to that effect gaderit all that he might in Fyfe Angus Streerne Stirllingschyre and the haill wastland and come to Stirling witht the number of ten thowsand men quhair bischope James Bettone mett him witht all the gentillmen of Fyfe and thais accompaned witht him to the effect foresaid and also the Master of Killmaris come to him out the wast , Kyle , Carrick, Cunninghame, quhilk was in number 2000 men, and tuk his wangaird in hand to come fordward to the toun of Edinburgh.

Bot the Earle of Angus knawand this nobill man the Earle of Lennox gadderis and aganis him witht bischope James Bettoun and the Master of Killmaris and hearand that they war of greit of number knew weill it was nocht done by the kingis adwyse quhairat he was greatlie astoneist . Zeist Nochtwithstanding he tuic sic curage and hardement that he knew weill thair was no remedie bot ether to do or die, and send incontinent to all his kin and friendis and in spetiall to the Lorde of Home and Ferniehurst and the laird of Cesfurde, also he send to the Lord Hamilltoun schawand his enemies the Earle of Lennox was to come witht ane airmie to tak the king from beseikand him that he could quhilk was ffor his awin weill; sayand gif that the Earle of Lennox owercome him that the nixt day he wald do siclyde witht him, thaifor best it war to debait witht baitht thar powaris and strengthis in tyme' Of this desyre lord Hamilltoun was weire weill contentit and promist to metitt the Earle of Angus witht all his kin and friendis at Lythtgow. Bot on the morne efterhend the Earle of Lennox come out of Stirling witht thre great ostis marchand forwart to Edinburgh thair sett fordwart his porpois and intent quhilk he had taine in hand at the Kingis command.

Sa schone as the Earle of Angus knew of thair coming he went and schew the King the maner of how it stude, desyrand his grace gar mak procliemation baitht in Leytht and Edinburgh that all maner of man betuix sextie and sexten zeiris sould ryse incontienent to follow the King and debait his grace. They hierand thir wordis of the earle of Angus and knew the matter how it stude gaif bot lyttill ansuer agan wnto the Earle of Angus. The Earle seand that the King was slaw in the matter wist weill thair was nothing bot ether do or die and thairfor maid him manfullie to the fieldis and caussit his friend Archibald Douglas, provost of Edinburgh to ring the common bell and put the toun in order and command thame to ryse and come witht the king in all haist to defend him aganis his enemis and left his brother George witht the king to cause him ryse and come fordwart for to support him ffor he wald pase incontient forward to meit the Lord Hamilltoun quho was abone Lythgow in redynes witht ane great number of 2000 men , and the Earle of Angus himself witht the Homes and the Karis quhilk was in the number of 2000 men. Be this the word come to the toune of Edinburgh that the Earle of Lennox was withtin ane myle to Lythtgow witht thrie greit ostis to the number of 12,000 men well furnist witht artaillze, and was porpossit to come to Edinburgh gif he war not stopit. Then George Douglas heirand his desyrit the King right effectouslie for to ryse and passé fordwart to help his brother and support him aganis his enemeis schawand how neirhand they war bot the kingis grace tuik lyttill thocht o the matter an was werry slaw in his fourtht ryding. Bot at last the post come from the Earle of Angus schawand the baitht the airmeis was in sight of wther and was purpossit to fight, thairfor prayand the kingis grace to come fordwart witht the toun of Edinburgh to reskew the Earle of Angs or ellis he wald be lost be ressone of the number of the wther pairtie. Then the King gart blaw his trumpetis and lap on horse and gart ring the common bell of Edinburgh commanding al maner of men , so ischit fourtht of the wast port and all the toun of Edinburgh and Leytht witht him the number of 3000 men and raid fordwart to the craigis of Costorphin. They had the artaillze on baitht the sydis lykis it had bane thunder. The George Douglas cryit on the King beseikand his grace for godis saik to ryde faster that he might reskew and help his brother. Be this the post come and schew the King that baitht the fieldis war iunitt and fightand furieouslie witht wther on the wast syde of Lythtgow tua mylieis be wast the toune and that the Earle of Angus and the Earle of Glencairneis was zokit togither and the Lord Hamilltounis and the Earle of Lennox in lyke maner and baitht fightand furieouslie. Then the King raid fast to sie the maner bot incontinent thair mett him ane post schawand to him that the Earle of Lennox men war fled frome him an he beleift that he had tind the feild. Bot then the King was werie sorrie and cryit on all his serwandis and all the wald do for him to ryde to the field and stanche the slaughter, and in spetiall to saif the Erle of Lennox gif he could be comprehendit allvue. Witht this the kingis serwandis and sindrie gentillmen passit at the kingis commandement , witht Andro Wood o Largo quhilk was the kingis commandement and ane of his famellear serwandis and carwer to him, and at that tyme haisit thair horse allis fast as they might beir thame, to the field to keip the kingis commandment to saif all frome slaughter and in spetiall the Earle of Lennox quhom he fand lyand slaine in the deid thraw cruellie be Schir James Hammilltoun that tyrane efter that he was taine in the field be the laird of Perdiffan and his wappouns taine fre him. In this meane tyme Schir James Hammiltoun that cruell murtherar gart schut him fre his takoris and thair slew him withtout Marcie and did so witht all that he might owertak that day in the field. Their war money market that ay witht his mark. Bot we will returne to Androw Wode and the kingis serwandis quho raid suoftlie throw the feild to saif all freindis that thay might comprehend on lyffe quhill at last they fand the Earle of Glencairne still fightand witht 30 men leift of all his airmie on lyue wnslaine and fled frome him, bot zeit was in sic ane strength that his enemis might on nawayis war him sa lang as he had ony men left on lyue to defend him. Bot inmedeatlie Androw Wode the Kingis serwand tuik him and saiffit him in brocht him away on lyue and conwoyit him to ane quyit place quhair nether the Doglassis nor the Hammiltounis might comprehend hin to do hin skaitht. This beand done the kingis serwandis come throw the feild and saw the Lord Hammilltoun standard murnand beside the Earle of Lennox, sayand 'The wyssist man ' the stoutest man the hardiest man that ewer was brede in Scotland was slain that day' and tuik his clok of Skarlat and cust it wpoun him in gart watchmen to stand about him quhill the kingis serwandis come and bureit him. This matter beand finischit and money slaine and taine on baitht sydis and in spetiall the Earle of Lennox witht money gentillmen of the Wast land witht him and in lyke wyse the Earle of Glencairne ewill wondit to the deid and money of his friendis and serwandis slaine and allso sum gentillmen of Fyfe baitht taine and slaine to wit , the Laird of Lethine slaine witht money wther gentillmen taine. This cruell and wnhappie feild was striking in the zeir of god Im V XX[127] zeiris and in the moneht of September

---

127 Translated incorrectly - this should of course read 1526.

Appendix 4
Full version Of Leslie

Efter certain monehis, Lenox of the handis, to this end with a chosen armie of mailed men of weir cam to Lithgw. Angus perceyeung his mynd, sendis to Arran and prays him for ald kyndes constantile conformit betuene thame , to meit Lenox at Lithgwe him selfe with he Kingis shortliesa be thair with a gret force weil preparit. Arran in haste was readie, suner nor men beleiuet : and with a great power in Lythquow was presenet of September the third. Bydeng heir a lytle he sendis to Lenox , and prays him to desist, gif he refuse, he will nocht esteem him his sister sone but his enimie and ennimie to the realme.

Quhairfor he warnis him to respecte his awne well and his honour, and as his freindis in kinde and blude, sa he receyue a friendlie admonitoune :This admonitone Lenox wald nocht heir bot furiouslie ansuered, til Edinburgh he wald cum and ther suld he be or die be the way; Arran thocht this ouer proud a ansuer til his syster sone: quhairfor quhom he culd not lay with wordis, he labouris to stay with swordis: an nocht bydeng the Kingis cuming with Angus, metis Lenox on the west syd of Lythkwe quhair creullie tha 30k with spear, sword and gunn, gret slauchter, her specialis ar slane Erle of Lenox selfe, and the laird of Houstoun, with many ane Lenox his parte. The rest fled and chaipet. Angus with the King , quhen the field was fochtane, came to Lythquowe, quha lang afor the field had cum, gif the king had not finzet hin selfe seik, and cam out of the Castel of Edr mair with compulsione nor pleasure, and giv his hors had not of sett purpose, bein slaw in the way, The slawness of the Kingis horsmaid George Douglas in sik of furie, that with word and wand the Kingis horse he sharplie drawe out the gait and at last was sa wod that he spairet nocht proud wordis to the Kingis selfe. This iniure the Kings sourlie laid til his charges eftirward and forzhet nocht, quhen he banishet him.

Appendix 5
Memorandum from Albany to Du Prat

There follows a memorandum sent by Albany to Du Prat the chancellor of Francis I describing the outcome of the Battle of Linlithgow. It is interesting to note the numbers quoted, especially the conservative estimates given to Lennox's force, and the insinuation that he was ambushed. It appears Albany was being liberal with the truth in order to give Angus a bad name. The rest of the text goes on to discuss how the pro English Douglases can be usurped from power. The reference to the garrison at Dunbar is interesting as this is Albany's main enclave in Scotland manned by a French garrison.

Reprise of the Memorandum by Albany to the Chancelor [Du Prat] for Francis 1, [November Decenber1526], Teulet I, 69, H.iv 2539

Scotland is suffering from the violence and licence of Angus and his friends. James is learning to be profligate, greedy and wicked; and he cannot escape from their hands. Lennox gathered some men to join with Margaret, the chancellor [Beaton], Argyll, Moray and others; but Angus was aware of it , and along with Arran, his chief enemy, collected six or seven thousand men , with whom he surprised Lennox and his force of over four thousand, Lennox himself being among the slain. Angus is set upon destroying the house of Lennox and has deprived the chancellor of his estate and office, and treats all partisans of France in a like fashion. He has surrounded the King, fourteen years of age, with a murderous and wicked crew without reference to parliament. If Francis would preserve the old alliance and avail himself of Scotland he should represent the case to Henry and Wolsey through Jean Joaquin, especially as Henry is interested in the safety and welfare of one of who is so near to the English crown.

If Henry will permit Albany to visit Scotland, Francis might order him go and redress the matters, returning at once after putting James and the government in Margaret's hands with a satisfactory council named by the estates, Margaret being placed in possession of her jointure on condition that Henry does not receive or support in England Angus and his adherents. Francis may bind Albany on pain of forfeiture not to exceed his instructions and to return at the stated time.

If Francis approves, Albany will deliver Dunbar to persons chosen with advice of Margaret and the said council; the castle had better be thrown down than fall into English hands.

I Francis sees his way to offer Henry a defensive peace for the three kingdoms without condition he will know how to put the …………will satisfy France. Meanwhile as time will be necessary and the present juncture is not suitable, Francis will perhaps think it well to send for news of James, and also in the interest of Lennox's children, supported by a request from Aubigny, in considerations of the services rendered by the household of Aubigny to Scotland. The envoy should have credence to James and the estates of the bishops of Aberdeen, Argyll, Moray, and others advisable: Margaret should also have full instructions suitable of the estate of the affairs.

Margaret, the chancellor and other party should be asked in particular what they are prepared to do, and whether they are satisfied that Margaret and their council should govern; also on what Albany is expected to do, If he is sent, the guarantees offered, and the persons upon whom to rely, with assurance under their seals, and information as to whether actions are to be secret or notified to the people or estates.

Hopes of marriage in terms of the treaty of Rouen should be held out, Albany to enlarge upon the subject when he goes.

The proposed envoys will be able to take fresh supplies of victuals and powder, maintain hope in the garrison of Dunbar and deliver his pension to the captain with encouraging letters. Unless steps are taken the place will be put into the hands of the English, who will obtain the alliance they have always sought as soon as Angus and his party can convene the estates, although they could not convene them in requisite form or conclude any agreement of importance without the consent of the said estates and of Albany who they have not yet discharged of his office ; and they could not discharge him without giving him due notice.

As the duke understands that, if Henry desires a marriage between James and his daughter, his demand will be granted, it will be well to take prompt measures and affect a breach between Angus and Arran. , otherwise the Franco Scottish alliance is lost. Francis should consider this. The English are trying to isolate James from his friends and have him at their will.

As the English may not have the goodwill to grant what Albany has suggested, Francis will perhaps keep this project to himself, if he does not expect acceptance, and will devise some scheme independently. Meanwhile he should send to Scotland secretly and make sure of Dunbar.

The duke recommends the despatch of M. de Saignes with a herald who has been continually in Scotland; the sooner the better.

Appendix 6
Walking the Battlefield

We are fortunate enough to have good access to the battlefield by means of a heritage trail which runs along the east bank of the Avon; however land either side is private. The going is leisurely and to tour the field will take an hour to an hour and a half. Unfortunately it is currently impossible to make a circuit without extending the walk for another couple of miles up stream until you reach the aqueduct carrying the Union Canal at which point there is a steep climb up to the tow path and circuitous route back into Linlithgow along the busy Torphichen Road. We can only hope that when the quarry site is no longer deemed profitable, the owners will restore the land and provide access for a safer and more pleasant circuit.

Park the car at the Bridge Inn at Linlithgow Bridge. The pub serves good food and a pint and is an ideal base to plan the walk ahead or reminisce on your subsequent findings. Make your way across the new Linlithgow bridge taking the opportunity to peer over the parapet and appreciate the problems Lennox men would have had fording the river at this point. There are also fine views of the viaduct from here. To the west behind the pub is Manuel Hill, which dominates the approach to the bridge and a likely position for Lennox's artillery. Looking East along the main road it is difficult to discern the contours of the land as they are now covered in housing. Cross the bridge and at the traffic lights turn right along Mill Road. It is somewhere along this road that Arran would have drawn up his guns to protect the bridge's approach and perhaps build a barricade to offer the gunners some shelter. Then take the next right down to Burgh Mills. Just before the beautifully restored buildings of the mill itself you will find a footpath signposted as the heritage trail leading off to your left down the side of the first mill house. Be warned this is slippery when wet. It takes you under the arches of the viaduct towering above you. Once down the slope and against the river, it is time to take stock.

As you walk south, the slopes of Peace Hill reveal themselves to your left. It is easy to get overwhelmed by the man made slope created to support the railway and access the quarry. But as you move along the natural contours become easier to see. I suspect that the slope you see today is much steeper than that of 1526 but the change in height is discernable and gives you a good idea of the problem Lennox faced in attacking it. Note also the ground. The ground is still marshy despite the presence of the quarry now filled with water. The field to your left is crisscrossed with drainage ditches and marshy burns. Even after a fair summer the land in September retains a spongy texture.

As you walk south, the wasteland at the foot of Peace Hill gives way to the quarry site. Beyond the water rises the slope up to the Torphichen Road. It gives a clear sense of the amphitheatre into which Lennox advanced. Also make a mental note of the distance to the rising ground. It is the funnelling affect of the terrain here that nullified any advantage Lennox had in numbers. Arquesbus and Cannon could easily disrupt the advance from the ridge but it is hard to imagine that rolling boulders would cause too much hardship.

To your right across the other side of the Avon is well drained farm land which in 1526 was water meadow. The meadow rises up to the Whitecross road and Manuel Haugh Farm. Beyond the farm the buildings of Whitecross can just be made out on the ridge line.

The woodland along the river bank you are now walking through has been a noted feature on all the early maps and there is no reason to think that it was not in a similar state on the day. However the course of the river has shifted over the years. It is easy to imagine Arran's men using it as cover to watch the enemy move towards the Nunnery on the far side of the meadow, taking the odd pot shot every now and then to keep them on their toes. Likewise, Lennox's horsemen may have ventured along the West bank to look for a good crossing point before driving the Hamiltons away from the ford at the nunnery.

The King's Fountain The oldest working fountain in the United Kingdom, The King's Fountain stands in the courtyard of Linlithgow Palace. Commissioned by James V in 1538, and erected under the custodianship of James Hamilton of Finnart. Finnart fell from grace just after the completion of the work at Linlithgow and was tried by his peers for the most part for the murder of Lennox and the treasonable role he played in the battle. (Authors Collection).

After about 1½ kilometres the field on the west side of the river peters out and nestled in the trees on the far bank towers the gable end of the Manuel Convent. It is quite an impressive and unexpected sight. The boulders and rocks that are strewn around the riverbank mark the remains of the convent and, unless you walk in winter when the river is at its highest, it is difficult to believe that the building was torn down by the power of the flooded Avon. However the 6ft banks suggest the river can run very high and fast. Take a minute to contemplate that the cemetery for the Nunnery lay traditionally on the south side, that is to say where you are now standing !

Looking back along the way you came, you can now really imagine the task that lay ahead of Lennox when he crossed the ford at Manuel. To the east lies a water meadow now some 300 metres wide before it rises up to the sprawling Woodlescote Farm. If you advocate the theory that the battle was fought at Peace Hill with the adversaries facing North - South then you will appreciate the march that Lennox's pikemen now faced. Hemmed in by the ridge and the river with the small holding of Drum ahead the chances of keeping your formation would seem limited.

Alternatively if you favour the East West disposition of the forces then the ridge up to the works surmounted by its chimney stack would be your obstacle, lined with Hamilton's troops albeit thinly.

For those of you wanting to return for the pie and pint at the pub it is now best to start back north retracing your steps. Otherwise it is onwards past the very impressive remains of Manuel Mill on the far bank and climb up onto the Union Canal aquaduct. Once at the canal, walk east until you meet the Torphichen Road Come back into town along the road. Unfortunately it's a busy road, so take care

As you make your way back along the road you will pass the salvage works on your left and approach the roundabout for the Kettlestoun Estate. All along this road across the fields to your left,are the best views of Peace Hill, the valley floor and the crest which Arran defended. It is a fair walk from the convent to the foot of Pace Hill even today but imagine this over boggy ground, carrying an 18ft pike, then charging up hill into the face of those guns and into the hedgerow of pikes at the crest. It is hard to believe that Lennox's men made it that far!

Finally the road brings you out at the roundabout at Kettlestoun estate. On the far side of the road you will find The Lennox Cairn. Somewhere in the estate of modern houses lies the true spot of his murder. The road into town past the Rugby club is the probable approach of Douglas's men, Andrew Wood and eventually the King.

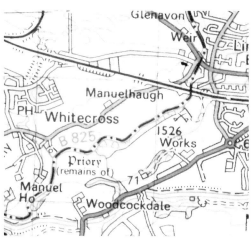

OS Map of Linlithgow Bridge

Take the road opposite the cairn and you are back on Mill Road. To your left is the crest of Peace Hill, Arran's chosen fighting ground. Take a minute to view the approach from Arrans point of view and ask yourself what you would have done in his position as he watched Lennox's flank march develop. Now pass under the railway and you will find yourself back at the Linlithgow Bridge, the Inn and that well-earned pint.

Of course once rested, you can always complete the tour by walking into the historic town of Linlithgow itself and visit the great hall at the Palace where undoubtedly the victors of Linlithgow celebrated their hard won victory in style. However, I don't advise riding a horse into the Loch !!

Appendix 7
Retinue Badges of the families at Linlithgow Bridge

Although open to a certain degree of debate, the following heraldic tinctures and emblems are associated with the families and would have been likely candidates for retinue colours and badges.

Family or Clan	Retinue Colour (Primary Tinctures)	Badge / Symbol
Lennox	White / Red	Red rose or Bulls head
Bethune (Beaton)	Blue	Otters Head
Galbriath	Red	Bears head
Scott	Yellow / Blue	Stag
Cunningham (Glencairn)	Black / White	Unicorns head
Maule	Red / White	Escalope
Kennedy / Cassillis	White / Red	Castle or Dolphin
Elliot	Red / Yellow	White Heather / Baton
Argyl	Yellow / Black	Lymphad or Galley
Moray	Red	Mullet / Star
Homes	Green	Lions Head
Hamiltons	Red / White	Cinquefoil / Oak tree with a saw through it
Kerrs	Red / White	Kerr Knot
Stirling	White / Black	Buckle
Douglas	Red / White	Heart
Wood	Red	Oak tree
Home	Green	
Ross	Red	Sprig of Juniper
Sempill	White and Red	Hunting Horn
Lindsay	Blue and White	Lime Tree
Linlithgow Militia		Black Bitch

Appendix 8
Source Material

Record sources and collections of correspondence

- Accounts of the Lord High Treasurer of Scotland 1473 - 1566. Ed Thomas Dickson and Sir James Balfour Paul (Edinburgh 1877 - 1916)
- Acts of Parliament of Scotland, edd T. Thomson and C. Innes (Edinburgh 1814 - 75), vol ii (1424 - 1567)
- Criminal Trials In Scotland from 1488 to 1624" Ed. Robert Pitcairn, (Edinburgh 1833) Bannatyne and Maitland Clubs 1829 - 1833
- Exchequer Rolls of Scotland 1264 - 1600 Ed J Stuart et al (Edinburgh 1878 - 1908).
- Letters and Papers , Foreign and Domestic of the reign of Henry VIII (Vaduz, 1965.)
- Letters of King Henry VIII, a selection with a few other documents Ed M St Clare Byrne (Cassell 1968)
- Letters of King Henry VIII, 1526-29 : extracts from the Calendar of State Papers of Henry VIII. (Norwich : Stationery Office, 2001.)
- Letters of James V, 1513 - 1542 Edd R.K. Hannay and D. Hay (Edinburgh 1954)
- Papiers d'etat…relatifs a l'histoire de l'Ecosse au XVI siecle Ed. A Teulet (Bannantyne Club, 1852 - 1860)
- Registrum Magni Sigilii Regum Scotorum edd JM Thomson et al (Edinburgh (1882 - 1914)
- Registrum Secreti Sigilii Regum Scotorum Volume iii (1513 - 154), edd J.B. Paul and J.M. Thomson (Edinburgh 1884)
- State Papers of Henry VIII (London 1830 - 1852)

Primary Sources:

- 'A history of Greater Britain, as well England as Scotland' by John Major (Edinburgh : T. & A. Constable, 1892.)
- 'The Anglica Historia 1485 - 1537' by Polydore Vergil Ed and trans by Denys Hay, (Royal Historical Society London 1950)
- A Diurnal of remarkable occurrences that have passed within the country of Scotland since the death of James IV till the year 1575' (Bannatyne and Maitland Club, 1833)
- The Expecdicion into Scotland of Edward, Duke of Somerset 1548' By Patten
- The Historie and Cronicles Of Scotland - Vol 2" by Robert Lindsay of Pitscottie trans JG Mackay (Scottish Text Society 1899 - 1911)
- The Historie Of Scotland - Vol 2" by Jhone Leslie Ed Thomas Thomson (Bannatyne Club 1830)
- "The History of Scotland" - by George Buchanan trans J Aikman (Glasgow and Edinburgh 1827 - 29) vol ii
- The History of Scotland" - by George Buchanan trans unknown 1821 edition
- 'Rhoit or Quhell of Tyme' by Adam Abell NLS MS 1746, see Alasdair m Stewart, " The Final Folios of Adam Abell's'Rhoit or Quhell of Tyme' in Janet Hadley Williams ed Stewart Style 1513 - 1542 Essays on the court of James V (East Linton 1996)
- 'History of Scotland from the year 1423 until the year 1542' by William Drummond of Hawthornden (London Edn 1681)
- 'Picturesque antiquities of Scotland' by Adam De Cardonnel (London: : Printed for the author, and sold by Edwards, in Pall-Mall; also at Edwards's, in Halifax., M,DCC,LXXXVIII. [1788])

Main Secondary References:

- 'Anglo Scots Wars' By Gervase Phillips (Boydell Press 1999)
- 'Armies and Warfare in the Middle Ages' by Michael Prestwich (Yale University Press 1996)
- 'The Art of Warfare in the Sixteenth Century" by Sir Charles Oman (Greenhill Books first published 1937)

- 'Commentaires' Monluc, Blaise de Lasseran-Massencôme, seigneur de
- 'Crown Magnate Relations in the Personal Rule of James V 1528 - 1542' by Jamie Cameron (Tuckwell Press 1988)
- 'The Douglas Book' by W.Fraser (Edinburgh 1885)
- 'Episodes in West Lothian History' by AM Bisset (Dundee 1928)
- 'Flodden, 1513' Niall Barr (Tempus 2001)
- 'Flodden, a Scottish Tragedy' by Peter Reese (Birlinn 2003)
- 'History of Scotland from the Accession of Alexander III to the Union -Volume iv' by Patrik Tytler (Edinburgh 1864)
- 'The History of Scotland from the Accession of the House of Stewart to that of Mary' by John Pinkerton (Edinburgh : printed by James Ballantyne and Co. for Bell & Bradfute; William Laing; Doig & Stirling; William Blackwood; and Oliphant, Waugh & Innes, 1814.)
- 'History of the Scottish People from Earliest Times' by Rev. Thomas Thompson
- 'History of the Town and Parish of Linlithgow' by G Waldie 3rd Edition Published 1879
- James V - King of Scots' by Caroline Bingham (Collins 1971)
- 'Margaret Tudor - Queen of Scots' by Patricia Buchanan (Edinburgh Scottish Academic Press 1985)
- 'The Lennox' by W Fraser (Edinburgh 1874)
- 'My Wound Is Deep' By Raymond Campbell Paterson (John Donald Publishers 1997)
- 'On a Tudor Parade Ground' by JR Hale (London - Society of Renaissance Studies, 1978)
- 'Place Names of West Lothian' by A MacDonald (Edinburgh, 1941.)
- The Renaissance at War' by Thomas Arnold (Cassell & Co 2001)
- 'Scotland and War' by Macdougall (Edinburgh : John Donald, 1991)
- Scottish Weapons and Fortifications 1100 - 1800' by DH Caldwell (Edinburgh John Donald 1981)
- 'Scottish Arms Makers' by Charles Whitelaw (London, Arms and Armour Press 1977
- 'Scotland, James V to James VII' by Gordon Donaldson (Edinburgh History of Scotland Vol iii -1965)
- 'Statistical Account of Scotland 1795' by Sir John Sinclair (Wakefield EP Publishing 1979)
- 'The Steel Bonnets' George Macdonald Fraser (Harper Collins 1971)
- 'Stewart Style - Essays on the Court of James V' by J Williams (East Linton 1996)
- Two Men in a Trench: Battlefield Archaeology - The Key to Unlocking the Past by Neill Oliver and Tony Pollard (Michael Joseph - 2002)
- The Triumphant Reign of Kyng Henry VIII' by Edward Hall ed Charles Whitby and T.C. Jack (London 1904)
- 'The Use and Effect of Weapons; The Scottish Experience' by David H Caldwell

Website:
Past Perfect: the virtual archaeology of Durham and Northumberland:
http://www.pastperfect.info/index.html